ART TREASURES
FOR AMERICA
SAMUEL H·KRESS COLLECTION

ART TREASURES FOR AMERICA

AN ANTHOLOGY OF PAINTINGS & SCULPTURE

IN THE SAMUEL H · KRESS COLLECTION

Prefaces by JOHN WALKER, Director of the National Gallery
of Art, Washington, and GUY EMERSON, Art Director of
the Samuel H · Kress Foundation

One hundred and eighty-seven Illustrations: Commentary
by CHARLES SEYMOUR JR, Professor of the History of Art,
Yale University

Φ

PUBLISHED BY THE PHAIDON PRESS · MCMLXI
FOR THE SAMUEL H · KRESS FOUNDATION

THE FRONTISPIECE IS AN ENLARGED DETAIL
FROM PLATE 57

BOOK DESIGNED BY LUDWIG GOLDSCHEIDER
© 1961 PHAIDON PRESS LTD · LONDON SW 7
BLOCKS ENGRAVED BY SCHWITTER AG · BASLE
PRINTED & BOUND BY VSK PRINTERS · BASLE
MADE IN SWITZERLAND

SAMUEL H. KRESS
Portrait painted by Leopold Seyffert

INTRODUCTION

THE Samuel H. Kress Collection had its beginnings in the third decade of this century, when the man whose name it bears was becoming known as one of our country's great merchants. The life of Samuel H. Kress is a typical American success story. Born in Cherryville, Pennsylvania, in 1863—almost a hundred years ago—he began teaching as soon as he had finished school. With his savings from seven years in this profession, he was able to purchase a small stationery and novelty store, which succeeded so well that he was soon thinking in terms of a group, or chain, of stores. This was not an entirely new idea. One or two chains were already operating in the North. But for the South it was a pioneer venture and quickly proved a most successful one. The first S. H. Kress & Co. emporium, which opened in Memphis, Tennessee, in 1896, met so patently a need in the area that Kress stores were opened in one city after another and profits multiplied.

Partly for business reasons, partly for enjoyment of the fruits of his success, Mr. Kress made frequent trips to Europe. Visiting the great European museums again and again in the course of his travels, he developed a taste for art and had already become a collector on a small scale when, about 1920, he met Count Contini-Bonacossi in Rome and was fired with the idea of emulating the Count in the formation of a private collection. It was only some years later, with the establishment of a lasting friendship with Bernard Berenson in Florence, that he decided to concentrate his collecting in Italian painting and sculpture.

The fabulous acquisitions of American museums in recent years and the great numbers of American tourists that now crowd transatlantic ships and planes every summer make it hard for us to remember how little of European art was to be seen in this country in the 1920's and how few Americans were then traveling abroad. Mr. Kress saw a challenge in this situation. With the same insight that had enabled him to recognize in 1896 the need in the Southern states for popular stores, he now recognized the need in America for more of the cultural advantages that art could afford and he set himself the goal of meeting that need in the domain of Italian art.

He had a vision of forming a collection in which every important Italian artist would be represented, so that Americans unable to visit Europe could study and enjoy a comprehensive selection at home. How well he succeeded may be judged from the observation made by Mr. David K. E. Bruce, President of the National Gallery of Art, at the time of the first Kress donation to the Gallery, in 1939: "Experts state that there is no private collection in the world, and few museums, which can illustrate in as complete a manner as the Kress Collection the development of the Italian school of painting and sculpture during the Renaissance period."

It was in this year, 1939, that Mr. Kress decided what disposition he would make of the paintings and sculpture which now filled to over-flowing his New York apartment. How he was persuaded to give up his plan to build a Kress Gallery in New York and how he came to feel that his collection would be more effective if he sent it to join other collections in the National Gallery, then under construction in Washington, is told in fascinating detail in Mr. Walker's note (see pp. XIX ff.).

When Mr. Kress made the donation and saw his paintings and sculpture installed in time for the opening of the National Gallery of Art, in 1941, he did not look upon the Kress Collection as complete. He planned to supplement it and to heighten its quality through new gifts and loans over an indefinite period of years, and he had begun to carry out his plan when he developed an illness which kept him an invalid for almost ten years before his death, in 1955.

Mr. Kress had years before made provision for the continuation of his philanthropic activities. In 1929 the Samuel H. Kress Foundation was established "to promote the moral, physical and mental well-being and progress of the human race". Beyond this general statement of purpose, Mr. Kress did not stipulate the scope of the Foundation's activities. He

CLAUDE W. KRESS
PORTRAIT PAINTED BY LEOPOLD SEYFFERT

left its Trustees free to make grants wherever they might see fit, but obviously his underlying purpose was to provide a facility for the development of the project closest to his heart, the field of painting and sculpture. The same flexibility characterizes the extensive funds left to the Foundation by a brother, Claude W. Kress, upon his death, in 1940.

Now, when Samuel Kress's illness prevented his directing his business and philanthropies, his responsibilities fell upon the shoulders of his youngest brother, Rush H. Kress, who was made President of the Board of Trustees in 1946. When I became a member of the Board, in December 1947, I found that one of the principal problems then facing us was that of deciding whether further attention and funds should be devoted to the Kress Collection in the National Gallery. Rush Kress was at this time deeply absorbed in public medical projects, to which the Foundation has from time to time made munificent contributions, especially for postgraduate training. He was also impressed by the magnitude of his brother's initial gift to the National Gallery and was at first inclined to go no further in this direction. He was willing, however, to give the matter a hearing. We met with the officers of the National Gallery, where we found in the Director and the Chief Curator, Mr. David E. Finley and Mr. John Walker, masters of persuasion, and in the Administrator, Colonel Harry McBride, a man who spoke Mr. Kress's own language. When Mr. Kress realized that his brother had intended to do more for the Kress Collection in the National Gallery, he dropped any opposition he may have had. He studied the problem, and laid before the Foundation Board a project for carrying out his brother's intention. Soon he was thoroughly engrossed in the project and in its execution his merchandising experience was invaluable, for he showed great skill in purchasing paintings and a remarkable sense of what people would like. We are thankful now that his will prevailed even when opposed in some of the purchases, especially in the case of certain German and Baroque paintings.

The situation in America with regard to art had changed since the Kress Collection was originally planned. Many people were now going abroad and much European art was being acquired by the larger American museums. Exhibition space was becoming limited, even in the recently built National Gallery. It was therefore decided not to enlarge the National Gallery's total Kress Collection but to concentrate upon enriching it.

The famous Gustave Dreyfus Collection of bronze medals, plaquettes, and statuettes—more than 1300 items—which Rush Kress had acquired for the Foundation, was added to the Kress Collection at the National Gallery. But for the most part the decision not to enlarge the collection was followed. With close cooperation between the Foundation and Gallery staffs, the Kress Collection already at the Gallery was carefully classified, so that only the examples of painting and sculpture most needed there were retained and the rest were gradually returned to the Foundation. At the same time the Foundation began watching for opportunities to buy replacements which would meet the Gallery's needs in a distinguished manner.

RUSH H. KRESS
Portrait painted by Leopold Seyffert

XI

This program, pursued in the succeeding fifteen years, resulted in the acquisition of many of the finest masterpieces now in the National Gallery.

Simultaneously with the project of improving the National Gallery's collection there evolved, as a natural corollary, the project of forming what we designate as regional gallery collections. That this second undertaking should reasonably develop out of the first is explained by the return to the Foundation of part of the collection originally sent to Washington and by the Foundation's purchase of much more from which to choose replacements in the National Gallery's collection. In this way a large number of works of art became available at the Foundation for distribution elsewhere. The choice of the other recipients was determined by the very simple and human desire to make some return to certain cities for all they had done for the Kress Company. The eighteen that have received regional collections are Allentown, Pennsylvania; Atlanta, Georgia; Birmingham, Alabama; Columbia, South Carolina; Denver, Colorado; El Paso, Texas; Honolulu, Hawaii; Houston, Texas; Kansas City, Missouri; Memphis, Tennessee; Miami, Florida; New Orleans, Louisiana; Portland, Oregon; Raleigh, North Carolina; San Francisco, California; Seattle, Washington; Tucson, Arizona; and Tulsa, Oklahoma. The requirements to be met by the recipient museums were few: permanent gallery space was to be provided; the galleries were to be fireproof, air-conditioned, and humidity-controlled; the paintings and sculpture were to be properly lighted and tastefully arranged; and, above all, none of the objects was to be kept in storage but all were to be permanently on exhibition for the education and enjoyment of the entire community.

Before there had been any announcement of our plan for regional galleries, I visited the eighteen designated cities to discuss the project with the museum directors. Their reactions were as various as their personalities—incredulous, skeptical, or enthusiastic. Now, after years of friendship, we often laugh together over the experiences of those early days; for they were the prelude to a remarkably close cooperation between the Foundation and the museum concerned in each project. The museum director and his associates were consulted in all matters and they played a dominant role in choosing their collections. So strong was the local enthusiasm for the project that not only were the requirements of air-conditioning, lighting, etc., fully met, but in most cases either a new wing was built for the Kress regional collection or a whole new building was inspired.

Every effort was made to keep the quality of the regional collections high. Some estimate of how high it is could have been formed by anyone witnessing the extreme reluctance with which scores of the paintings, for example, were released by the National Gallery. Moreover, the Foundation sometimes made special purchases in order to emphasize certain phases of the regional collections being formed; and in the never-ending effort to strengthen and enrich the collections, changes were frequently made in them even after they had been installed.

As the consultations and resultant selections progressed, constant and arduous work of restoration and framing was carried forward, the Foundation assuming responsibility for the good condition of all the objects and for the suitable framing of the paintings. Our remarkable collection of nearly eight hundred original Renaissance frames purchased in Italy was put at the disposal of Italian master framers who, like the group of expert restorers, worked under the direction of Mario Modestini, a distinguished connoisseur and one of the most skillful restorers of our time.

Then came the packing and shipping, which developed into something of a science. Even though many sensitive panel paintings, which ideally ought never to be moved, were included among the hundreds of objects shipped over many thousands of miles, our staff can take pride in the fact that very little significant damage has occurred.

By the time each collection had been installed, a special local catalogue was ready for distribution. The notes were written chiefly by the late William E. Suida, who for many years devoted to the Foundation his vast store of knowledge and his great gift for research. But the catalogues were joint productions; for not only did the local directors sometimes supplement

Dr. Suida's notes with their own commentaries, but the local museums directed and financed the press work.

Finally, there came the Opening Day, with generous and hospitable ceremonies and functions provided by the local staff and Board of Trustees and participated in by Mr. and Mrs. Kress, the mayor of the city, the governor of the state, the Foundation staff, and distinguished citizens. These occasions won valuable public cooperation for the museums and wide publicity, toward which the local newspapers contributed handsomely.

While some of the regional collections have gone to museums already richly endowed, others have brought fine paintings and sculpture into communities where almost nothing of the kind was to be seen before. Most gratifying has been the reponse to the donations. They have increased museum attendance, have proved useful to neighboring schools and colleges, and have stimulated local citizens to make generous gifts to their own institutions. Favorable comment on the regional-gallery project has come from all quarters. One Paris journal, for example, ran a series of articles advocating a study of the project and its adoption in Europe.

After the regional gallery collections had been formed, there still remained, in what the Trustees designated as a Study Collection, over two hundred paintings and a few pieces of sculpture. These have now been given to universities and colleges which would otherwise have little or nothing beside reproductions to illustrate their courses in the history of art. One group of paintings was given to Ponce, Puerto Rico, thus the collection now extends from Puerto Rico to Honolulu and from Miami to Seattle.

In addition to the preceding categories, significant donations have been made by the Kress Foundation to the Metropolitan Museum of Art in New York and to the Philadelphia Museum of Art, almost wholly in the field of decorative arts. Remarkable among the gifts to the Metropolitan Museum are the superb French furniture and porcelains collected by Lord Hillingdon and the beautiful Adam Room from Croome Court, country estate of the Earls of Coventry. The gift to Philadelphia is a series of tapestries with scenes from the Life of Constantine after designs by Rubens and Pietro da Cortona. Originally from the Barberini Palace in Rome, and then separated for many years, these tapestries are now reunited to serve as decoration for the great hall in the Philadelphia Museum.

Kress benefactions have not been confined to America. Samuel Kress found means of expressing his gratitude to Europe also for the enjoyment her treasures and monuments afforded him in his travels and for the works of art he was permitted to buy and bring to America. It was in restoration projects that he saw his best opportunity to help, for he had become increasingly aware of the precarious condition to which much European art had been reduced through the erosion of time and neglect. Among the important edifices in Italy which he restored wholly or in part through his personal philanthropy, he loved most of all the Palazzo Ducale (Gonzaga Palace) in Mantua. It was his custom to visit it each year in the month of September, and its curatorial and custodial staff looked forward eagerly to his coming. Even now, more than twenty years after his last visit, members of the staff tell of his kindness to them and of his affection for this strange and beautiful palace with its miniature suites and private chapels built for the dwarfs whom the Dukes of Mantua kept for entertainment.

The Foundation, following as usual the pattern of Mr. Kress's philanthropies, has assisted in the restoration and preservation of other important monuments in Italy and has extended the work to Greece and Turkey, and especially to Germany, where Nuremberg, the ancestral home of the Kress family, has been extensively aided by Kress Foundation funds in its post-war restoration.

Finally, in view of the interest in a wide dissemination of the benefits from the Foundation's philanthropies, it was inevitable that some funds should be devoted to publication. The first major undertaking in this field was *Signs and Symbols in Christian Art*, a book inspired by Rush Kress's desire to aid in the understanding of Christian religious art, which constitutes a large portion of the Kress Collection. The book, published in 1954, is generously illustrated with reproductions in color of paintings in the

Kress Collection and with supplementary line engravings of individual signs and symbols.

Closely related in purpose to *Signs and Symbols in Christian Art* is *The Four Gospels and the Acts of the Apostles*, a Foundation publication of 1959, in which the King James version of the Biblical text has been arranged and printed by Richard Ellis to conform in beauty to the many illustrations, again taken from the Kress Collection.

The broader field of art history also is being aided by generous publication funds from the Foundation. It was a Foundation subsidy which financed, in 1952, a revised edition of Berenson's famous essays, *The Italian Painters of the Renaissance*. The handsome volume, with its numerous illustrations, is not only a help to students and lovers of Italian art, but, appearing while both the author and Samuel Kress were still living, it fittingly celebrates their long friendship, in which Rush Kress also shared. As Berenson's essays were accompanied in their early editions by the author's no less famous lists, *Italian Pictures of the Renaissance*, so the Foundation has assumed the subsidizing of a new edition of the lists, in several volumes, all being published, as was the volume of essays, by the Phaidon Press. In this series the two volumes on the Venetian Schools, with over 1300 illustrations, was issued in 1957, two years before Berenson's death. The other parts of the series, which will include four more volumes, with thousands of illustrations, had long been in process of revision by the author and are now being made ready for the press.

Another distinguished scholar of Berenson's generation, William E. Suida, was honored by the Foundation's publication in 1959 of *Studies in the History of Art*, a volume to which more than fifty specialists contributed in honor of Dr. Suida's eightieth birthday. Happily this book was off the press several months before Dr. Suida's death brought an end to his long and brilliant career, the last twelve years of which were dedicated to the Kress Foundation.

Now that hundreds of Kress Collection paintings, sculptures, drawings and objects of decorative art are installed in the institutions to which they have been donated, the Foundation has undertaken the publication, in seven volumes, of a comprehensive catalogue, to cover the whole collection. This catalogue will include, along with reproductions of all the art objects, a revision of pertinent data already published in National Gallery and regional-gallery catalogues and will add all available information and documentation on the many objects not included in these previous publications. The seven volumes will thus cover more than 1500 paintings and sculptures, over 1300 small bronzes, and many examples of decorative arts.

The present *Anthology* is designed to serve as an introduction to the seven catalogue volumes, which are to follow as rapidly as possible in the next few years. We have called this introductory volume an anthology, in pleasant allusion to the Greek derivation of the word: *anthos*, meaning flower; and *legein*, to gather. In gathering the flowers of European art, the Foundation has not limited its selection to orchids. For this introductory volume we have not confined our choice to what we regard as "best" nor restricted our selection to one or two schools of art. Rather, our purpose has been to give a summary view of the quality and scope of the whole collection. The Italian, Dutch, Flemish, French, Spanish, Portuguese, and German schools are represented here, covering a period of six centuries. Interspersed among masterpieces by such great artists as Giorgione and Dürer are productions by many lesser masters. Indeed, the extensive representation of the so-called minor masters in the Kress Collection was a matter of pride with the founder, as it has continued to be with his successors; and it is interesting to note that Samuel Kress's early appreciation of the minor masters antedates the general awareness that their grace, lively interest, and quiet power account in no small measure for the appeal of Renaissance art.

Simultaneously with the publication of this *Anthology*, an exhibition is being held at the National Gallery of Art in Washington. There, along with the National Gallery's Kress Collection, is shown a selection from all the regional-gallery collections. The full measure and quality of the Kress gift to the Nation is thus amply displayed.

Having been in charge of the Foundation's art project for fourteen years, I cannot but regard it with enthusiasm. When one has concentrated on an absorbing task for nearly a decade and a half of one's mature life, there is, of course, some danger of losing a true perspective. To avoid attacks of "art astigmatism" I have found it helpful to consider great European picture galleries like the Uffizi, in Florence, or the Prado, in Madrid. Such comparisons remind me that we should have started collecting during the Renaissance, when the great Masters were taking commissions, and when the kings of Spain could order masterpieces by the dozen.

We cannot hope to compete with the great museums of Europe and we have not tried to compete with anyone in building up the Kress Collection. Yet we need make no apologies. The National Gallery in Washington is, in many respects, the most beautiful museum in the world, and the Kress gift is an ornament to it. Splendidly exhibited as the Kress Collection is there and elsewhere, it cannot fail to be a perpetual source of enjoyment and an inspiration to further collecting. We are confident that the National Gallery and the other museums with which we have had the pleasure of working in recent years will continue to build up their collections in quality and beauty, and we hope that this book will serve as a record of our close cooperation of some fifteen years' standing.

I wish to express the great appreciation of the Kress Foundation for the help of many people in producing this volume. Our special thanks go to the staff of the National Gallery of Art, to Professor Charles Seymour for his excellent text and his help in selecting the illustrations, and to the directors and staff of the Phaidon Press for their tireless and devoted work over a period of two years in the production of the book. I should like especially to extend my personal thanks to the entire staff of the Samuel H. Kress Foundation.

GUY EMERSON

A NOTE ON THE KRESS COLLECTION
AT THE NATIONAL GALLERY OF ART

THE Kress Collection and the National Gallery of Art are practically contemporary. Though Samuel H. Kress began buying works of art as early as the 1920's, the most important purchases were made partly by him and partly by his brother, Rush H. Kress, between 1937, the year the Gallery was founded, and the present. With its bold and rapid buying, the Samuel H. Kress Foundation became a dominant factor in the international art market and in twenty years formed a collection of amazing beauty and significance, in many ways unique in the history of collecting.

It was an exciting experience to take some part in the Foundation's quest to try to find paintings and sculptures which would help to build up a great National Gallery in this country. In 1938 I was appointed Chief Curator of the new Gallery. A prior commitment to the American Academy in Rome prevented my assuming my duties immediately, but during the summer I came to America to consult with the Director, David Finley, about plans for the building. When I arrived, ground had already been excavated. I remember seeing a sign which imposed a speed limit of five miles an hour for trucks moving inside the excavation. I was appalled. The collection of the Founder, Andrew Mellon, was all the Gallery possessed. How could it be stretched through a building of such immensity? This problem had not troubled Mr. Mellon. He had faith that if he provided a large and beautiful museum building, its effect on works of art still in private collections would be magnetic.

Nor did it trouble Mr. Finley. He believed that the very selectivity of the Mellon Collection, with its extraordinarily high quality, would keep people from realizing that we were trying, with only 152 works of art, to fill a building that covered two city blocks. I alone seemed to anticipate complications. If the Gallery opened with only this collection, would Congress, like nature, abhor a vacuum? And would tremendous pressure be exerted to fill these acres of unoccupied exhibition space? It seemed to me that the Trustees of the Gallery might well find such pressure intolerable.

Perhaps I was needlessly apprehensive, and, actually, Congress has never been anything but helpful in its relations with the Gallery. In any case, if any danger existed, it was averted. The Gallery received unexpected, but vital help. Two lovers of art, Jeremiah O'Connor, then Curator of the Corcoran Gallery of Art, and Herbert Friedmann, Curator of Birds at the Smithsonian Institution, had for some years spent their leisure together, intent on their favorite pastime, seeing as many private collections as possible. In the winter of 1938 they visited the Kress Collection in New York. They left dazed by the splendor of what they had seen. On his return to Washington Mr. O'Connor wrote Samuel Kress urging him to give his collection to the new National Gallery. The letter argued strongly against private museums and pointed out that the pledge of the United States Government to provide funds for the support of the new institution offered security for the future of the collections. It was an eloquent appeal and must have been effective. The correspondence was continued, and on April 18 Mr. O'Connor conveyed to Mr. Finley an invitation to call on Mr. Kress.

The meeting revived an old acquaintance. David Finley and Samuel Kress had once crossed to Europe on the same ship, but with characteristic modesty Mr. Kress had scarcely mentioned his collection. When Mr. Finley saw what treasures had been brought together at 1020 Fifth Avenue, he realized the importance of the collection to the National Gallery. He had arrived at 3 p.m.; he left at 10 p.m. During those seven hours, with his inimitable powers of persuasion, he induced Samuel Kress to give up his plans for a private museum, for which property was already under option, and to consider giving most of his collection to the National Gallery.

In the end Mr. Finley and I were permitted to choose about two thirds of the paintings and sculpture in the Kress Collection, partly for the permanent collection of the Gallery and partly for a study collection. This amounted to 416 paintings and 35 pieces of sculpture. It must have been very hard for Samuel Kress to face parting with all of these; for in many ways his paintings and sculpture were to him a substitute for the children he never had. He loved them tenderly, and it was a great joy to us to know that he was happy about the way they were eventually displayed in the National Gallery of Art. About once a month Mr. Finley and I would go to New York, and Mr. Kress would walk with us on the terrace of his penthouse or sit with us in his living room, where the blank walls seemed to accuse us of the treasures that had been removed. We would discuss the collection: how it looked, how it could be improved. Even in the last tragic years, when he was almost completely paralyzed, any mention of the National Gallery of Art stimulated him to the effort of a reply.

It was Samuel Kress's wish to strengthen the Gallery wherever its collections were weak. Subsequent to his first donation, he acquired enough paintings by Watteau, Fragonard, Boucher, and other French artists of the period to fill two galleries; and at the time he became ill, in 1945, he was purchasing pictures to fill other gaps. The last painting David Finley and I spoke to him about was the great canvas by El Greco, representing Laocoön and his sons. Prince Paul of Yugoslavia had sent this to America before the outbreak of war, and the Kress Foundation was able to buy it at a price which then seemed immense, but which now seems relatively small.

After Samuel Kress was stricken with an illness which, though resisted for a number of years, removed him from all activity, his brother, Rush Kress, with wonderful dedication took over the presidency of the Samuel H. Kress Foundation and devoted much of its resources to collecting for the National Gallery and for eighteen other galleries throughout the country. For a decade after the war the art market received an influx of important works. During these years it was a "buyer's market". It is difficult to believe that comparable opportunities will come again.

A number of paintings had been sent across the ocean to the United States for safekeeping, among them the great round panel of the *Adoration of the Magi* from the Cook Collection in England. It seemed to me the most important art refugee in America, but the price was very high. Rush Kress hesitated to commit such large funds to a single purchase. We went together for one last look at the picture, which was about to be crated in readiness for its return to England. The label on the painting read "Fra Filippo Lippi", but I explained that Bernard Berenson had published an article in an Italian periodical years earlier proving that the picture was largely by Fra Angelico, Fra Filippo's master. I proudly added that, as a student, I had helped B.B. (as Berenson was known to his many friends) gather data for his article.

B.B.'s theory turned the tide. To my joy, at the last possible moment Mr. Kress decided to buy this and several other pictures from the Cook Collection. He asked me to see Mr. Berenson on my next European trip and to tell him the Kress Foundation would like to publish his article in English in a lavishly illustrated monograph with many color reproductions. I said I knew B. B. would be delighted, and I would arrange everything. When I arrived at the Berenson villa, I told B.B. of the wonderful acquisition, and he agreed that it was one of the most beautiful paintings in the world. But when I mentioned the proposed republication, he looked at me, holding his head in his hands, and said, "Nothing must be reprinted. I was mistaken. The picture is almost entirely by Fra Filippo Lippi." Today the painting is labeled, I believe correctly, as by Fra Angelico and Fra Filippo Lippi, for technical examination after the cleaning of the picture seems to confirm B.B.'s original theory, but his article has never been republished.

Sometimes my persuasion, sometimes David Finley's, sometimes Stephen Pichetto's, or William Suida's, or Mario Modestini's interested Rush Kress and the Foundation in this or that work of art; but more often than any of us, it was Guy Emerson, Art Director of the Foundation, who succeeded and to whom credit should go for the extraordinary development of the Kress Collection. We were usually all in agreement about the most significant purchases, but there were occasions when Mr. Kress had to persuade at least some of us that we were missing an opportunity. For example, when I first saw *Mary, Queen of Heaven* by the Master of the Saint Lucy Legend, the panel was so obscured by dirt and yellow varnish that I thought the picture problematical and the price too high. We looked at it repeatedly, for in those days there was very little competition, and we had plenty of time for decisions. After each inspection Mr. Kress would repeat his opinion that I was making a mistake. Finally, he bought the picture against my advice, and when it was cleaned and hung in the Gallery, it turned out to be, from the point of view of color, the most brilliant painting in the whole Flemish section. My chagrin was far outweighed by pleasure in Mr. Kress's triumph.

At his instigation dealers went abroad to try to shake further treasures from the golden orchards of the great European collections. This resulted, above all, in magnificent acquisitions from the Czernin and Liechtenstein Collections. Moreover, whatever of outstanding importance came on the New York, London, or Paris markets was likely to be offered first to the Kress Foundation, and the purchases in these years altered the character of the Kress Collection. Samuel Kress had been ambitious to have represented in the collection every Italian artist active from the thirteenth through the eighteenth century. He sought avidly the minor as well as the major painters and sculptors. With his withdrawal a change in focus gradually took place: more masterpieces were purchased and less attention was paid to the minor Italian artists. The schools north of the Alps received new emphasis. A room devoted to the German masters was assembled; two rooms of early Flemish and Hispano-Flemish paintings were added; two galleries of seventeenth- and eighteenth-century French paintings supplemented those Samuel Kress had given; and Spanish, Dutch, and later Flemish pictures were bought for the Gallery.

Between 1945 and 1956 there were similar changes in the collection of sculpture. An important group of fourteenth- and fifteenth-century Italian sculpture from the Liechtenstein Collection was added, as well as the beautiful Annunciation group by Nino Pisano. The tabernacle by Desiderio was bought from the Alphons de Rothschild Collection, and the bust of Francesco Barberini by Lorenzo Bernini, from the Barberini Family. The French eighteenth-century section was especially enriched with pieces by Falconet, Pajou, Clodion, Houdon, and others.

One of the most important single acquisitions was the collection of medals, plaquettes, and small bronzes assembled by Gustave Dreyfus, the greatest modern collector in this field. These have been installed in specially designed rooms. The gift of the Dreyfus Collection ranks the National Gallery of Art, as a center for the study of Renaissance bronzes, with the museums in Florence, Vienna, Berlin, and London.

Some idea of the magnitude of the purchases made by the Kress Foundation between 1945 and 1956 may be gained from the Kress exhibitions held in 1951 and 1956 to commemorate the tenth and fifteenth anniversaries of the opening of the National Gallery of Art. In the two exhibitions there were 208 paintings and 46 pieces of sculpture. From these two shows the Kress Foundation offered the National Gallery the choice of as many works of art as would strengthen and enrich the collections in Washington. This gift was one of the most munificent ever made to any museum. In exchange the Gallery returned all that it could spare from the Kress Foundation's previous gifts and loans.

The Kress Collection includes more than a third of the works of art on view at the National Gallery of Art, where it now fills 34 galleries and consists of 365 paintings and 82 pieces of sculpture and 1307 medals, plaquettes, and small bronzes. Of the original gift from Samuel H. Kress there remain 122 paintings and 9 pieces of sculpture in the National Gallery. Those no longer in Washington are now among the treasures distributed to other museums throughout the United States.

The Kress gifts to the National Gallery of Art and to other museums are witnesses to the formation of one of the great collections of our time. While only a part of the magnificent assemblage is presented in this anthology it nevertheless serves to indicate the high level of excellence in this remarkable donation to the American people.

JOHN WALKER

ART TREASURES FOR AMERICA

AN ANTHOLOGY OF PAINTINGS AND SCULPTURE
IN THE SAMUEL H · KRESS COLLECTION

ART TREASURES IN THE KRESS COLLECTION

Nella mia mente potei far tesoro.
DANTE, PARADISO I.

THE pageantry surrounding the presentation of a comprehensive collection of Western Art, as in this volume, has an allure all its own. So much is encompassed between two covers. Even if you may not hold, in the poet's phrase, 'infinity in the palm of your hand', you may imagine for a moment what it might feel like to do so. And, as tokens of more than six centuries of inspired sensitivity and grandeur flutter beneath the fingers with the turning pages, it might appear very nearly possible to glimpse 'eternity in an hour'.

This is part of the magic of books. That spell, nevertheless, should not be allowed to overshadow the enduring power of the work of art itself, or of the tradition to which it may belong. No verbal description, no reproduction can ever take the place of seeing a painting, a piece of sculpture, or a great building in the original. A work of art has physical presence—like ourselves. It is not only a bulwark against pedantry and banality. It may also prove to be an insurance against our own particular twentieth-century brand of spiritual loneliness, and it can be looked on as a constant teacher in helping us to see what is around and within us—clearly and with a discriminating eye.

'Of my mind may Thou make a treasure house': this is one way of translating the epigraph in Italian at the head of this essay. The words come from Dante's prayer at the beginning of the last stage of his cosmic journey described in the *Divine Comedy*. In context, the passage echoes the poet's need to remember in order to communicate what he has been privileged to 'see'. But the same prayer has meaning for any one who approaches a work of visual art. We see truly and fully only what the mind is prepared by experience to receive. Dante's prayer in the *Paradiso* might be inscribed over the doors of our museums. For the true treasure-house is not the museum alone, but ultimately the mind of each visitor. Strangely and paradoxically, a volume of this kind, which is a preparation for experience, may most help the reader by asking him to start to cease to be a reader and to look for meaning in the forms of painting and sculpture more than in words. It offers him wherewithal to add to the treasure-house of the mind, not for storage but to draw upon for seeing.

But seeing itself seems to depend upon customs and standards of a moment. What is recognized as art may vary considerably from generation to generation, and from century to century. There are works of art included in this volume which almost certainly would not have been selected a hundred years ago except as curiosities or as rather daring forays into Ruskinian 'primitivism'. Up to 1850 on the North American eastern seaboard one would have found only sporadic imports of painting from Europe and a taste still dominated by respect for Greco-Roman forms. An English visitor, who on the whole was well pleased with his transatlantic sojourn in the late 1830's, was shocked and amused to find in a prominent New England mansion a plaster cast of the nude *Apollo Belvedere* completely draped in cloth, 'in compliance', as it was explained to him, 'with general opinion'.[1] In this remarkable way the Puritan heritage coped with the doctrines of the German philosopher-historian Winckelmann, who in the eighteenth century set the standard of artistic excellence as the sculpture of Greece and Rome, and of the Italian sculptor, Canova, who translated Winckelmann's view of the Antique into whitest marble.

Americans for a while were content to accept these standards at second hand. They were seemingly quite unaware of the color and vitality of Medieval or Renaissance art which they mistakenly confused with what they called the 'bigotry' of the Old World.

Another wind was stirring. By the 1850's Nathaniel Hawthorne in his novel, *The Marble Faun*, was attempting to deal with a problem of meaning in which the Antique was to be seen not in early nineteenth-century New England isolation, but in an Italy that was still in places Medieval or Renaissance in spirit and in *mores*. In 1860 there was an even more dramatic evidence of change. Only three years after the pioneering exhibition of Italian 'primitives' at Manchester in 1857, there arrived in New York harbor one hundred and fifteen original paintings collected in Italy to show 'the progress of Art' from the Venetian 'Byzantine', so dear to Ruskin.

The collector who brought these pictures to the United States exactly one hundred years before the time of this writing was a Bostonian, a son of the developer of Sandwich glass, and before going to Italy, the editor of the first English-language newspaper in what is now the State of Hawaii. His name was James Jackson Jarves. His aim was not just to amass a collection of Italian painting to illustrate, as it were, the history of art. It was to bring evidences of an art, which had never been seen in so extensive and complete a way by an American, to his native land so that the citizens of the rapidly growing republic might become acquainted with representative originals on their own soil, in their own environment.

This bold adventure in ideas was unfortunate in its timing. The outbreak of war in 1861 had a naturally dampening effect. There were suspicions of the paintings' quality, and even in some instances of authenticity. One by one Boston, New York, Washington were eliminated as possible purchasers. In the end the pictures ended up in a southern New England college which had a newly dedicated art building in the 'Ruskinian taste'. Only over the next decade after the Civil War did the pattern of municipal museums in the large cities begin to take on life; and only gradually thereafter did the importance and charm of early Italian painting become recognized. Jarves was in his own country a prophet without honor for some time. But he was a prophet.[2]

In one of his still interesting and readable books about art Jarves predicted that in time private collectors would bring to North American shores so much of the art of Europe that the museums of our cities would equal those of Europe itself. This obviously has not occurred; the greatest things, the towering achievements of the Middle Ages and the Renaissance, cannot now be moved from long-established collections or from the places they were designed for and where, thank heaven, they have twice survived the dangers of modern war. But long before 1860, great altarpieces of earlier styles had gone out of fashion and had been removed, sold, or abandoned to moulder. Jarves himself was an eye-witness to the practice of selling old medieval panels for burning in order to recover the gold leafed on to their backgrounds. The nineteenth century was to a certain degree a century of dispersal and destruction, but it became also one of salvage which continues on to the present day with ever increasing knowledge and effectiveness. And though the stream of beautiful paintings of the Middle Ages and the Renaissance from Europe to our shores has all but dwindled to a trickle, the richness of our museums is indeed breathtaking. Jarves' ideal has proved far from a barren thought.

The formation of the Kress Collection, as outlined earlier in this volume by John Walker, Director of the National Gallery of Art, Washington, and by Guy Emerson, Art Director of the Samuel H. Kress Foundation, has been strikingly similar in intent, but on an unprecedented scale. No fewer than 1550 European paintings and sculptures have been brought together in the

Kress Collection. Many of the finest are in the National Gallery of Art: but other masterworks have found their way to museums across the nation (even as far as our newest State of Hawaii). This is in truth a citizen's collection in origin and a citizen's collection in its ultimate aim. The purpose of this Anthology is to offer a glimpse into the riches which have thus been made available in our own day to twentieth-century Americans.

It is against this background that we should approach the carefully selected group of some one hundred and thirty-five works of art from the great collection of European art that is the Kress Collection. The earliest painting chosen, a portentous image of the Virgin and Child [1] given to the Florentine, Giotto, belongs to the Age of Dante. It is perhaps not a coincidence that one of the earliest collectors of Italian 'primitives' of the thirteenth and fourteenth century, Artaud de Montor, was the author of a famous book on Dante. In our own

FLORENTINE PAINTER, ABOUT 1530
ALLEGORICAL PORTRAIT OF DANTE · WASHINGTON

country the foremost of the American nineteenth-century art historians, Charles Eliot Norton, was a translator of the *Divine Comedy*. In the Kress Collection is perhaps the grandest ideal portrait of Dante ever painted, from the hand of a Florentine painter of about 1530.[3] Huge in scale, broodingly thoughtful, the poet protects with one hand the Cathedral and Baptistry of his native city of Florence, above the flames of Inferno, while behind him are the cold sea, Eden-topped Purgatory and the unearthly glow of the spheres of Paradise. This combination of the transitory and the eternal, of the familiar and the strange, of the natural and the supernatural, is basic to our vision of Italian painting.

To Dante and his Italian contemporaries of the early fourteenth century the art of painting was dramatically renewed and definitively given a fresh and 'true' direction by the artist we know as Giotto. There was probably in this view a good measure of simplified thinking, perhaps even a kind of propaganda. Already in his life time Giotto was the subject of a legend. He appeared as the hero who single-handed turned tides of taste and vision. He was the new champion who vanquished the old. This metaphor of a knightly tournament is implied in Dante's famous lines from the *Purgatorio* in which the painter of the older generation, Cimabue, is said to have 'thought to hold the field; but now the cry is all for Giotto.' One can almost hear the crowd shouting for its favorite, as the gay pennons stream in the breeze and heraldic devices gleam in the sunlight! To Petrarch, Dante's immediate heir to the laureateship in poetry, Giotto's reputation was 'huge' *(inter modernos fama ingens est)*. He personified the optimistic and humanistic trends of the first half of the fourteenth century. He seemed, like Dante, to tower over his contemporaries as an *individual*, in the full sense of the term as we use it in our Western traditional way. The figure of Giotto, touched with myth as much as existing in historical fact, is an effective introduction to this survey of so many aspects of the Western tradition in art, for art is concerned with both history and myth.

The generation immediately preceding our own studied Giotto primarily through eyes which were the first to 'see' Cézanne. The bulky, structural aspects of his art were stressed above all

3

others. For a time sculptural and architectural allusions abounded in the writing about his painting. His forms were admired because they seemed to present something of the roughness and durability of granite or basalt. This was not true of the criticism closest to Giotto in time and spirit. Cennini, his spiritual great-grandson, and the author of a famous hand-book of medieval painting, wrote that Giotto 'had more finished craftsmanship than any one has had since'. Ghiberti believed that Giotto was 'great in the art of painting' because he abandoned the 'crudity' of the Byzantine manner and brought 'good taste to his study of nature, never departing from a correct sense of measure'. Pucci wrote that Giotto was 'subtle' *(dipintor sottile)*. Politian wrote that his 'hand was as sure as it was facile' *(quam recta manus tam fuit et facilis)*.[4]

An impression of sureness, suavity and measure strikes one first, on viewing the *Madonna and Child* [1–2]. The panel must have belonged to a very important altarpiece from which three other similar panels of saints survive. This altarpiece in turn must have come from the period of the frescoes in the Bardi Chapel in S. Croce in Florence, that is, somewhere in the latter period of the artist's career when he was experimenting with a new kind of delicacy and subtlety in color and expression. Cennini, who claims that he received the secrets of Giotto's technique in direct line through Taddeo Gaddi (Giotto's godson and his follower for no less than twenty-four years), speaks of the desirability of all possible finesse in modeling a head, urging the painter not to cover the preliminary shadow-layer painted in a dark neutral tint but to fuse the flesh tints with the shadows by the lightest conceivable touch, 'softening them like a puff of smoke'. It is almost as if one were reading of Leonardo's *'sfumato'*!

Look now at the Virgin's head. Although some of the accents have been reinforced, the feeling for a 'puff of smoke' is there. Against the abstract gilt ground the figures are not modeled out aggressively into space as in the Ognissanti Madonna of 1314 (now in the Uffizi) but are spread out and contained within the confines of a flattening plane, in harmony with the pervasive golden plane of the non-naturalistic background. Extreme richness of ornament is carried from the haloes into the decoration of the robes. And yet the grandeur and the superhuman scale are not impaired. This wonderful image illustrates Cennini's definition of painting which could well have come from Giotto himself: 'an occupation... which calls for imagination and skill

4

2. Head of the Madonna · Detail from Plate 1

of hand, in order to discover things not seen, hiding themselves under the shadow of natural objects… presenting to plain sight what does not actually exist.' The combination of the seen and the unseen, of the tangible and the intangible, is repeated in the echoes of the forms of Mediterranean Antiquity mingled with the Early Medieval interlace of line in ornament.

It is tempting to think of this *Madonna* as the central panel of the lost altarpiece of the Bardi Chapel, which we may assume was by Giotto and his very successful shop, or *bottega* of assistants. Only gradually did the Medieval and Renaissance methods of collaboration between master and assistants yield to the more purely individual design and execution we are used to in modern painting. Here, however, in this *Madonna* one may feel amply entitled to see the *magisterium*, the 'mastery' of a great directing mind. It is the painting in America which best illustrates Giotto's aims on a grand scale. The picture illustrates admirably one other traditional feat of Giotto's, namely, that he 'changed the profession of painting from Greek back into Latin'. This is an allusion to a decisive shift away from medieval Greek, or 'Byzantine', style which had become very popular in Italy in the thirteenth century.

The appeal of this 'Greek' kind of painting, rich with gilt and bright with colors approaching enamels or even jewels in brilliance and saturation, can readily be understood by looking at the *Coronation of the Virgin* by Paolo Veneziano, the Venetian painter of the highest reputation in the first half of the fourteenth century [3]. Venice, through trade, was more closely linked to Constantinople and the Byzantine world than any other Italian center. This picture is very important, for it is currently believed to be the earliest dated panel (1324) which can surely be ascribed to 'Paul the Venetian' and it shows him very much under the Byzantine spell. It is an art still heavy with ritual. It does not unfold a view identical to normal experience, but instead one which is parallel, at some distance, to daily life; it proposes an unearthly vision of dogmatic truth and confides a sense of the mystery of religious doctrine. Interestingly enough it is almost exactly contemporary with the *Madonna* which shows so strikingly the competing style introduced by the Florentine Giotto.

ANOTHER CENTER of strong Byzantine influence in Italy was Siena. The greatest exponent of the Sienese adaptation of the Byzantine was Duccio di Buoninsegna, a contemporary of Giotto's. Duccio's masterpiece was the *Maestà* or 'Majesty of the Virgin, enthroned with Saints and Angels' completed in 1311 for the High Altar of the Cathedral in Siena. The back of the altarpiece was decorated with much smaller scenes illustrating the Life and Passion of Christ. Some of these smaller panels were at one time detached from the altarpiece, and the *Calling of Peter and Andrew* [4], one of the great gems of the Kress Collection, is one of them. The element of a delicate and meandering line is at once apparent. It controls particularly the rocky symbolic 'landscape', and against it the figure of Christ which seems to float instead of to stand. The suggestion of the miraculous extends to the little cockleshell of a boat and the figures in it. The figures make a pattern in an abstract space; and against the gold background the gestures take on a terse and startling poignancy.

Along with the vigorous movement in Tuscan painting in the early part of the fourteenth century there was a counterpart in sculpture. Our American museums are far weaker in sculpture of the period than in painting. For this reason the beautiful pair of life-size statues carved in the full round of an *Annunciation* group [5–6] are particularly noteworthy. They belong to a *genre* of sculpture in wood, originally always painted, which Pisa, Lucca and Siena brought to a peak in the fourteenth century and continued deep into the fifteenth. The pair illustrated here repeat very closely the striking gestures and drapery-schemes of a pair in marble, in the Church

3. Paolo Veneziano · The Coronation of the Virgin · Washington

4. DUCCIO DI BUONINSEGNA · THE CALLING OF THE APOSTLES PETER AND ANDREW · WASHINGTON

of S. Caterina in Pisa, which Vasari, the sixteenth-century Tuscan biographer of artists, wrote of as by Nino Pisano, active toward 1350, whose style was less Florentine than Sienese in its grace.[5]

The lyrical possibilities of the Sienese style were particularly attractive to the late Medieval centers of painting north of the Alps. Actual journeys by Sienese painters such as Simone Martini to the papal court at Avignon, visited also by Giotto, helped to spread the style, which merged soon by affinity with the graceful courtly forms of Refined Gothic painting in France, the Rhineland and Flanders. By the end of the fourteenth century there had grown up a widespread manner of painting over most of Europe, from the British Isles to Bohemia and from Norway to Naples, usually called the 'International Style', in which Northern and Italian elements mingled harmoniously to mutual advantage.

8

5. HEAD OF THE VIRGIN ANNUNCIATE · DETAIL FROM PLATE 6

This trend came to full flower quite early in the fifteenth century. A beautiful example painted in Italy is the *Madonna* by Gentile da Fabriano [7] of about 1415 to 1420, pleasing in color and enriched with the most elaborate kind of punch-work and *sgraffito*-work in the gilded portions. One feels the presence of a great lady or a Queen in the figure of the Virgin. Rather than the 'International Style' it might much more graphically be called the 'Courtly Style'.

The richness and grace of Gentile's painting bears a direct relation to early fifteenth-century sculpture in Tuscany. One thinks of the earliest designs by Ghiberti for his 'First Doors' of the Florentine Baptistry and to some extent of the loveliest of all effigies of the fifteenth century, that of Ilaria del Carretto in the Cathedral at Lucca by Jacopo della Quercia. Quercia was an unsuccessful rival of Ghiberti's in the famous Competition, held in 1401–1403, to determine who was best fitted to make the Baptistry Doors. We do not know exactly what Quercia's

9

6. Nino Pisano · The Virgin Annunciate and the Archangel Gabriel · Washington

7. GENTILE DA FABRIANO · MADONNA AND CHILD · WASHINGTON

11

earliest work was like for lack of documented pieces, but a *Madonna of Humility* in the Kress Collection [8] has the swinging rhythms of 'soft' drapery, the Sienese type of the Madonna's features, and a sense of the possibilities of design in three dimensions that we associate with Quercia before he developed his most characteristic and personal Renaissance style toward 1415. The Kress piece is a great rarity, and projects in an unusually impressive way the combination of grace and serious beauty which the International Style might create at its best.[6] In Flanders, particularly in connection with the fabulously colorful court life of the Dukes of Burgundy, this sense of dignity mingled with elegance found a supreme expression in painting. Here we think primarily of Jan van Eyck but even more of the mysterious master of Flémalle, who may have been the artist recorded under the name of Robert Campin.

From a church in Bruges comes a large and impressive altarpiece of the *Virgin and Child with Saints* [9–11] which is to be identified with the style of the Master of Flémalle, but in a more

8. Jacopo della Quercia · Madonna of Humility · Washington

9. MADONNA AND CHILD
DETAIL FROM PLATE 10

10. Master of Flémalle and Assistants · Madonna and Child with Saints in the Enclosed Garden · Washington

precise and sharper vein than we normally associate with him. Here the Early Flemish love of naturalistic detail turns toward an elaborate system of overlapping and interlacing forms. Look for example at the pages of the book held by St. Catherine at the lower left; or at the hands of the Virgin as she clasps the Christ Child. The scene takes place in a walled garden, symbolic of the Virgin herself, the *hortus conclusus*. In the foreground a tapestry-like covering of plants and flowers, each endearingly portrayed from carefully observed specimens, prefigures Dürer and Leonardo. These plants symbolize the late medieval idea of the endless mystery and beauty of our world; they represent also the infancy of modern botanic science in art. The St. John holding the Lamb presents the same design as the St. John in the so-called Medici Madonna by Rogier van der Weyden, who was Campin's great pupil.

Little by little we are being taught to see and understand more clearly the regional variants of the 'International Style'. For example, in Italy, there was a tendency to retain a slightly more sculptural approach in the drawing and modeling of the human figure. In the North the figures tended to become weightless, as in the designs of the tapestries which were woven principally in Northern France and Flanders. Sometimes around these figures the space flattens out to imitate a tapestry also. This 'tapestry-space', as it might be called, took the fancy of at least one

14

11. FLOWERS · DETAIL FROM PLATE 10

12. GIOVANNI DI PAOLO · THE ANNUNCIATION · WASHINGTON

Italian painter, Giovanni di Paolo, whose *Annunciation* [12–13] contains at the left the scene of
the expulsion of our first parents from Paradise. The plants and flowers are arranged in a marvelously free flat pattern against which, like heraldic emblems, are to be seen two pairs of
delightful rabbits, symbols of the fleshly dangers of the world. Meanwhile, as one's eye moves
past the Annunciation scene, it comes to rest in the quite different spatial convention of a cubicle
which houses St. Joseph at the right. The 'cubicle-space' harks back to Giotto and the Sienese
before 1350. This ability to shift and choose styles of space is a remarkable aspect of Late
Medieval painting. We should think of it as an art of *virtuosi* rather than of 'primitives'.

There might be added here a number of other characteristics of this art. In the North of
Europe there was a continuing emphasis upon the goldsmith's art, and its influence on painting
must be clearly imagined if we are to see with any understanding what goal the painters were
working toward. Gold, laid on in thin-beaten leaves and then delicately engraved, was for a
long time used as a background for figures garbed in long, sweeping draperies of clear, bright,

16

13. THE EXPULSION FROM PARADISE · DETAIL FROM PLATE 12

contrasting and enameled color. The total impression is jewel-like [14–15]. The Kress Collection contains a little masterpiece of a *Crucifixion* by the anonymous Rhenish painter of the very early fifteenth century known as the Master of St. Veronica [15.] And closely related to the School of Avignon in France is a larger and somewhat later panel [14]. The figures of Christ and the Magdalen are seen in the dramatic confrontation scene which goes under the title given by the Savior's words, '*Noli me tangere*', of the Vulgate. [John 20:17, 'Jesus saith unto her, *Touch me not;* for I am not yet ascended to my Father.'] The precision of linear outline sets the actors off against the garden-world of the landscape. The painting could have been produced in Switzerland or even Bohemia as patently to our eyes as in France. Influence from Italy is nevertheless present. The Magdalen, for example, is quite clearly taken from Duccio's kneeling figure in the *Noli me tangere* of the *Maestà*.

A variant of this very effective flat-pattern style of painting is to be seen in the panel entitled *The Death of St. Clare* by an anonymous painter of quite definite individuality, called the Master of Heiligenkreuz from the Austrian monastery which was the source of the painting in which his style was first isolated [16]. The work of this painter is of the greatest rarity, and this example is one of only two to have come to America. The saint is shown at the moment of her death. Sisters of her Order attend her in prayer and one is about to lower the body upon the bed. Meanwhile angelic visitors swing censers and a group of saints headed by the Virgin, dressed like an earthly Queen, who closes the corpse's mouth, miraculously appear in attendance. Above, the skies open and Christ, surrounded by heavenly presences, receives the newly liberated soul in the guise of a crowned infant girl.

All of this narrative interest and closely observed characterization is organized in such a way that your eye catches without confusion what is going on once you are aware of the visual logic of presentation. The delicacy of execution, for example in the little musician-angels engraved directly on the gold background above the saints' haloes, constantly prepares surprises for a second glance. Tragedy and grief never emerge so strongly as really to disturb us, nor, it would seem, the medieval viewer either. The elongated proportions, the long, tapering fingers, the details of rich court dress, the jewels and brocade—all define a courtly ideal. The color and, above all, the line in its fascinating pattern carry not so much a story as the definition of a whole phase of European civilization.

To test the fact of the European-wide character of Late Medieval art it would be interesting to return to an Italian painting such as that by Giovanni di Paolo [12]. There will be found, I am sure, an underlying unity in spite of the surface differences of school and region. Giovanni di Paolo belonged to the Sienese School and was enrolled as a master in the painter's guild there in 1428. Roughly contemporary with this date is the peak of activity of an even more enchanting artist, whose qualities as an illustrator of the Franciscan legend were first brought out by Bernard Berenson in a famous study. This artist was Stefano di Giovanni, known as Sassetta.

A great altarpiece (dismembered by the mid-nineteenth century) devoted to St. Anthony Abbot was for a long time considered by his hand, a matter which since has become a topic of scholarly discussion.[7] James Jackson Jarves, whom I mentioned at the start of this essay, brought the first two panels from this altar to America. The Kress Collection contains no less than four panels from the St. Anthony Altar. The one shown here presents the visit of St. Anthony to St. Paul in the desert [17–18]. High at the upper left, the little figure of the saint makes his appearance, passes behind a hill, meets a pagan centaur whom he rebukes and converts to an amendment of life, and finally embraces his fellow saint in greeting in the lower foreground,

14. FRENCH PAINTER
EARLY 15TH CENTURY
CHRIST APPEARS TO ST. MARY MAGDALEN
AFTER HIS RESURRECTION
SAN FRANCISCO

15. MASTER OF ST. VERONICA · THE CRUCIFIXION · WASHINGTON

16. Master of Heiligenkreuz · The Death of St. Clare · Washington

21

17. SASSETTA AND ASSISTANT · THE MEETING OF ST. ANTHONY AND ST. PAUL · WASHINGTON

18. St. Anthony and the Centaur · Detail from Plate 17

having passed downward in the meantime through a gloomy wood, in miniature a recall of Dante's 'selva oscura' of the first lines of the *Divine Comedy*.

We may thus add as a last characteristic of the type of painting we have been examining an interesting suggestion of the lapse of time, with far-reaching psychological consequences. The eye makes a journey through the imagined world of the picture; its movement in harmony with the imagery makes possible the illusion of the passage of actual time; the time-element produces a feeling of authenticity in the narrative. And the narrative finally enriches the sense of spiritual experience.

With this lyrical kind of painting, which preserved a narrative style from the late centuries of Antique art, the Middle Ages in Italy produced their beautiful *cantilena* of departure. Our next illustration belongs largely, though not entirely, to another age.

23

19. Fra Angelico and Fra Filippo Lippi · The Adoration of the Magi · Washington

THERE is no discernible dividing line between the Middle Ages and the Renaissance. In fact, the latter term, as used to denote a metaphorical awakening and a new quickening of the spirit of inquiry, was not minted until the nineteenth century.

Nevertheless it is clear that by 1400, in Italy, there was a trend which appeared to open deeper perspectives and broader horizons of human life. One can hardly say that this was a 'discovery' of the heritage of Greece and Rome, for that heritage had never been entirely lost to sight by Medieval Europe. But it does imply that the Florentines particularly, among the humanists in Italy toward 1400, found new ways of using in literature and visual art surviving forms available to them from Antiquity. And this new capability helped mightily to open up a deeper appreciation of the natural world and to place a greater emphasis upon the idea of man's central place within that world. History, in the sense that Herodotus and Livy knew it, now became once more a major element of study and of cultural orientation.

In art, the evidence of this change was roughly contemporary with the appointment of a famous scholar from Greece itself to be the first professor of Greek at the Florentine center of studies and with Giovanni Villani's history of the Florentine republic in its relation to Italy. It was also contemporary with what has been rightly called a crisis in political and economic theory, in which, somewhat in ways we have ourselves experienced, it was a question as to whether a 'republican', citizen-enhancing framework for the state could survive the growing threat of more monolithic and autocratic forms. The first art in Florence to make a clear statement on this choice was the art of sculpture, which can make an image of a man for the actual space of squares and streets, or at entrances of important monuments. Thus was provided a new public imagery of man. The next art to follow was architecture, which provided a new kind of space. Last came painting. Here with the illusion of form in space, was the fusion of advances in figural and spatial art into a synthesis with an even more powerful appeal to the imagination. It could, and did, project a compelling vision of humanity as actor on a stage whose limits were considered not less than those of the world itself.

The large *Adoration of the Magi*, nearly five feet in diameter, is one of the great monuments of Florentine painting of the fifteenth century [19–21]. The picture appears to be identical with one mentioned as by the beloved Dominican 'Frate', the Blessed Angelico, in a late fifteenth-century inventory of the contents of the Medici house in Florence. While there may be an element of truth in this inventory's listing of the artist's name, it does not provide us with a conclusive answer to the question of the painting's authorship. What the picture seems to reveal is a fascinating combination of at least two major styles of art and the collaboration of representatives of two generations of artists.

In the foreground are the patterned plants and blossoms of Late Medieval 'tapestry-space'. In the background to the left is an arch of the Early Renaissance through which pours a multitude of people in attitudes of eagerness and amazement. Each one of them strives to occupy a portion of simulated physical space. Each seems to have weight and character. They do not exist merely—they act. Their movement pushes forward to the more isolated group of the Madonna and her Child with St. Joseph. Then, and only then, do you become aware of the subject of the picture as you recognize in the central kneeling figure one of the Wise Men, or Magi, who has dismounted to pay his homage to the long-awaited Savior. To the right, along a city-wall (not unlike that still standing today between the Porta San Giorgio and the Porta San Niccolò in Florence) a group of women and children echo the human aspect of the divine family in the foreground, as they admire in wonder the retinue of the Three Kings advancing from the mountainous area of the deep background. Their counterparts at the left are semi-nude boys and

young men who look as if they had just emerged from the athletic *palestra* of a Roman bath. Huge in scale, gorgeous in shimmering hues, a peacock is placed over the stable at the apex of a suggested triangle, and stamps the whole scene with splendor and with beauty.

Thus, while there are deposits of the late Gothic International style there are also touches of more closely observed human behavior and appearances and a sympathetic view of humanity in the large. Some of the figures could be derived from those on Ghiberti's bronze Doors for the Florentine Baptistry. Indeed, the challenge of combining great numbers of figures in a scene so highly charged with meaning both for the present and the past belongs to exactly the kind of artistic program that the '*Gates of Paradise*', which stand on the East side of the Baptistry, fulfill. Perhaps the part of Fra Angelico, who seems to have been influenced by Ghiberti, is largely in what would have been called the *disegno*, or determination of the general composition of the whole. The figures recall the style of Fra Filippo Lippi in some instances, and there are more than over-

26

21. MADONNA AND CHILD · DETAIL FROM PLATE 19

tones of the styles of such younger followers of both Lippi and Angelico as Pesellino and Benozzo Gozzoli. I do not know where the final answer to this art-historical riddle of attribution lies. But I do sense in the painting something of the situation uniting a master with younger followers such as one finds in some of Ghiberti's equally elaborate designs for this second pair of Doors for the Florentine Baptistry. And I would put the painting on much the same plane of idealism, and, allowing for differences of technique and civic function, of artistic achievement.

An opportunity for comparing the related, but still quite distinctive, personal styles of Fra Angelico, Fra Filippo Lippi, and Benozzo Gozzoli may be found in three panels characteristic of each artist's manner. Fra Angelico's *Healing of Palladia by St. Cosmas and St. Damian* [22, 24] comes from the predella of the High Altarpiece commissioned by the Medici for San Marco, in Florence (SS. Cosmas and Damian are the physician patron-saints of the Medici). It is the one painting in America which has the clearest claim to the hand of Fra Angelico since this most

22. FRA ANGELICO · THE HEALING OF PALLADIA BY ST. COSMAS AND ST. DAMIAN · WASHINGTON

23. Fra Filippo Lippi · St. Benedict orders St. Maurus to the Rescue of St. Placidus · Washington

important altarpiece with its whole series of *predella* panels is generally felt by specialists to be the master's work entirely. The detail in color presented here brings us close to the secret of Fra Angelico's method of painting. The domestic scene of the sick-room is provided with realistic touches of the gleaming ewer and basin and the homely three-legged stool near it. But the gestures of the saints, dressed in the fur-lined finery of their doctors' robes are delicacy and elegance themselves. The scene has dignity and intimacy; the effect of shadow does not disturb the contrast and harmony of bright colors with gold. Filippo Lippi's panel *The Rescue of St. Placidus* depicting an incident from the life of St. Benedict [23, 25] is less unified in its architectural setting but more sculptural in the figures. The detail presented here shows St. Maurus rescuing a younger saint from drowning. The emphasis is not upon the creation of a realistic setting for the action. It is quite the opposite. The scale of the natural world is reduced in order that there should be no competing element to obscure the gentle seriousness of the relationship between the two white-robed plastically realized figures. Benozzo Gozzoli in a similarly scaled *predella* panel *The Dance of Salome* [26] reveals a more precious, indeed jewel-like, linear depiction of form with an engaging use of simultaneous presentation of three scenes from the life of St. John the Baptist (again recalling Ghiberti's second *Gates*). The space of all these pictures is organized in a very loose approximation of one-point perspective. In this respect they do not precisely conform to the theory of painting put forward by one of the greatest of all Renaissance men, Leon Battista Alberti, in his treatise of 1435. But they do illustrate admirably his plea for clarity and dignity of form in relation to subject, for purity and harmonious contrast of color, and the attractive presentation of a dramatic narrative or, as he called it, *istoria*. 'The greatest work of a painter is not a colossus but an *istoria*,' he wrote.[8]

29

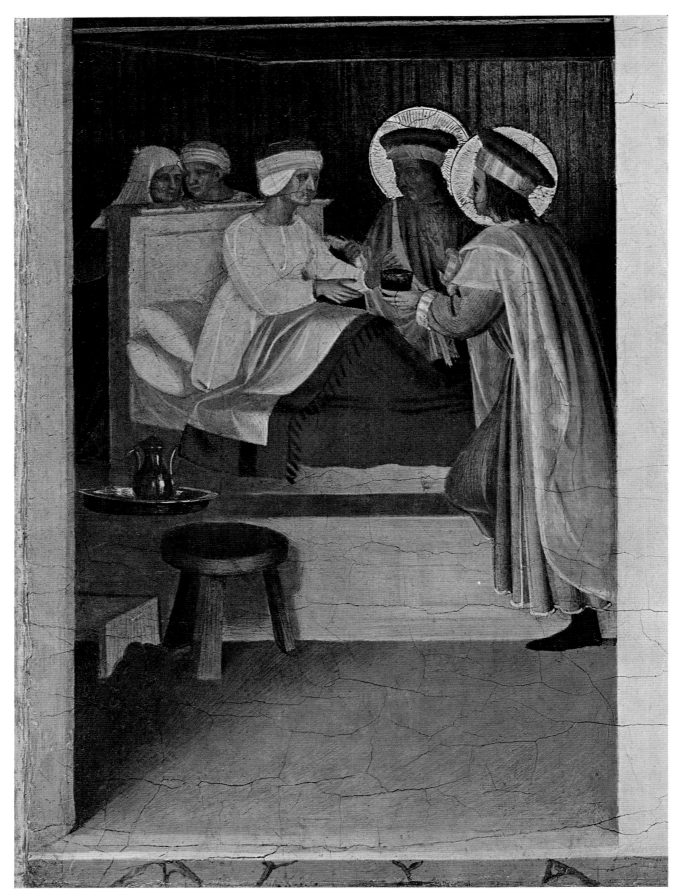

24. The Healing of Palladia · Detail from Plate 22

25. THE RESCUE OF ST. PLACIDUS · DETAIL FROM PLATE 23

31

26. Benozzo Gozzoli · The Dance of Salome and the Beheading of St. John the Baptist · Washington

A painting which reveals a respect for the Albertian system of mathematical perspective is the *Annunciation* [27] by an intriguing master, so far nameless, but called Master of the Barberini Panels, who apparently studied the work of Domenico Veneziano, Benozzo Gozzoli and Filippo Lippi. The cleanly carved architecture enclosing a marble-paved court, with its *loggie* and palaces, frames the figures and all but closes off the world of freely growing things glimpsed through the archway in the rear. Thus the *hortus conclusus*, the symbolic closed garden so dear to the Middle Ages, changed to the suggestion of an ordered closed square in the City of Man.

Alberti's concept of *istoria* in painting revolved about the vision of a meaningful action in a suitable setting. Like many Renaissance thinkers, he was interested not only in men but in mathematics. While he presupposed an unyielding mathematical system of order and proportion underlying all of nature, including man, to him beauty was not a static changeless perfection but an element of grace derived from harmony of movement, as much as of proportion. For him, such harmonious movement alone could express the beauty of soul within the painted figure. There was therefore in the tough and rigorous mind of the Renaissance thinker room for the poetic and more tender aspects of human feeling. A certain 'mode of revery' induced by ease of manner and what was called a gentleness of spirit [*gentilezza*] was indeed an aim of the Art which Alberti sought to see established; and perhaps understandably it was often in the creation of a space which was not rigorously and strictly ordered along the lines of a mathematical type of perspective that the mode of revery best succeeded.

27. MASTER OF THE BARBERINI PANELS · THE ANNUNCIATION · WASHINGTON

28. DOMENICO VENEZIANO · ST. JOHN IN THE DESERT · WASHINGTON

The truth of this last statement is well illustrated by two small predella panels from the most lovingly composed and beautifully painted altarpiece of the first half of the fifteenth century in Florence. This is the painting by Domenico Veneziano for the church of Santa Lucia ai Magnoli on the south side of the Arno in Florence, the parish church of Niccolò da Uzzano. Two of the saints surrounding the Virgin in the main panel, now in the Uffizi, are St. John the Baptist and St. Francis. Under the first, in the *predella*, was the panel of *Young St. John in the Desert* [28]. Under the second was the *St. Francis receiving the Stigmata* [29].

In the picture in the Uffizi, the figure of St. Francis is on the left extremity of the group surrounding the Madonna with St. John the Baptist next to him and at his left side. The predella panels must have corresponded in their *istorie* with the saints above, just as we find the system used in the statues and historiated reliefs under them of the church of Or San Michele earlier in the century. Thus the observer would have looked first at his left at the scene of St. Francis where

34

29. DOMENICO VENEZIANO · ST. FRANCIS RECEIVING THE STIGMATA · WASHINGTON

the organization of form is from left to right and leads the eye naturally to the *istoria* of the St. John [28].[9] The jagged shapes of pale mountains, seen almost as if by intense moonlight rather than by the usual light of day, define a landscape of the spirit. There, utterly alone, the nude saint, as if his image were inspired from an Antique statuette of a young Apollo, exchanges rich robes for the camel's-hair shirt of his new vocation. The gently modeled forms of the nude suggest the growing appeal of Renaissance Humanism in an environment still affected by ideas of Medieval asceticism. Here is a uniquely eloquent expression of the possibility of their reconciliation. Removed from the hurly-burly of life, garbed in cool tones of blue, green and rose, is the *Madonna and Child* [30] painted by Domenico for some private family in Florence, probably toward 1450. The background of a free pattern of blossoming rose bushes, the symbol of the Virgin as the 'rose without thorns', creates an environment of sensitivity and intimacy, and proposes a setting which was to have great popularity as a conventional solution in the succeeding

35

30. Domenico Veneziano · Madonna and Child · Washington

decade. The figures are sculptural with the humanity of Luca della Robbia and the purity of Desiderio da Settignano. No other collection in America contains as many as three panels by the rare master of form and mood who was Domenico Veneziano.

The second half of the fifteenth century in Italy presented two major directions in mood. One was contemplative and lyrical. The other was active and at times expressionist. We find both painting and sculpture sharing, each according to the opportunity accorded them as separate arts, in this double direction. The two arts ran parallel to each other and occasionally met to exchange effects.

The parallelism of Florentine painting and sculpture toward 1475 is seen in the two small *Madonnas* adjoining. The first [31], attributed to Rossellino's follower, Benedetto da Maiano, plays between forms almost in the round and the most delicate of flattened, or what we would

32. Desiderio da Settignano · The Christ Child · Washington

call 'painterly' relief in the background. With the two busts in marble, representing the Christ Child and the young St. John, the transition from the art of Domenico Veneziano's generation to a younger point of view is amply evident. The little *Christ Child* by Desiderio da Settignano [32] belongs to much the same kind of art as Domenico's. It is skilfully executed, lovingly observed, and closely related to the transient yet durable forms of life: the irrepressibly mischievous smile, for example, of an actual little child. The companion piece is similar in some aspects

33. Antonio Rossellino · The Young St. John the Baptist · Washington

of technique but quite different in spirit. It is less subtle in the transitions of one detail to another and more determinedly expressive of a mystical withdrawal from this world to another realm of religious or poetical imagination. The artist is presumed to have been Antonio Rossellino, one of the few fifteenth-century sculptors that Michelangelo is said to have admired sincerely. This *St. John* [33] reflects more than a little of the forms and quality of the art of the young Michelangelo.

39

34. CIRCLE OF ANDREA DEL VERROCCHIO (POSSIBLY LEONARDO DA VINCI)
MADONNA AND CHILD WITH A POMEGRANATE · WASHINGTON

Leonardo da Vinci, the greatest example of a universal genius of his times and perhaps of the whole of Western civilization, was trained as an artist in the thriving *bottega* of the goldsmith-painter-sculptor Andrea di Cione, called Verrocchio. There he learned the rudiments of painting and also it would seem certainly of sculpture, which he carried on later in his own individual and influential, but also quite inimitable style. The spirit of the early years of the activity of Verrocchio's workshop was not entirely the strong, energetic kind of art we think of in connection with Verrocchio's own style. There was room also for a quieter and elegant *gentilezza* to which undoubtedly the young Leonardo contributed the primary inspiration. Much of its exquisiteness is in the beautiful, delicately scaled *Madonna and Child with a Pomegranate* [34] which has been attributed alike to Leonardo da Vinci and his companion in the Verrocchio *bottega*, Lorenzo di Credi. The question of authorship should not obscure the jewel-like quality of this tiny devotional panel which is one of the treasures of the Kress Collection.

35. Domenico Ghirlandaio · Madonna and Child · Washington

If the *bottega* of Verrocchio was the great training place for the rising generation of artists growing up in Florence between 1465 and 1480, there must certainly have been an emphasis upon sculpture in almost everything that was done or discussed there. Another *Madonna* more obviously sculptural, the strikingly handsome *Madonna and Child* of Verrocchiesque cast [35], has been attributed to the young Ghirlandaio, whose training, like Leonardo's, was in the *bottega* of Verrocchio. This influence on the young Ghirlandaio, which can be traced into his

36. LORENZO GHIBERTI · MADONNA AND CHILD · WASHINGTON

37. DESIDERIO DA SETTIGNANO · BUST OF A LADY · WASHINGTON

later work, was more from stone-carving, it would seem, than from modeling in clay or casting in bronze. The firmness of the forms, expressed by a strong outline and definite modeling, might be compared with the softer forms and more yielding sentiment in a rarely beautiful *Madonna* in painted terracotta [36] which is attributed in the National Gallery of Art to the earlier Florentine sculptor, Lorenzo Ghiberti.[10]

The factor of technique, always important in sculpture, is made very clear here—in the way in which the malleable clay takes on a softer final form than would be the case in marble carved by the blows of a point or chisel. Look now at a piece of outstanding Renaissance marble carving in the portrait-bust of a young Florentine lady of about 1475 [37]. The bust has been usually given to Desiderio, but a few years ago it was proposed as an example of Leonardo's marble style and as a portrait of Simonetta, the beautiful relative of that Amerigo Vespucci, Florentine geographer and explorer, after whom the continents of the New World were to be named.[11] Whether or not one feels in the concept of the individual and in the style of execution the spirit and hand of Leonardo, these criteria of judgment certainly do not apply so well to Desiderio's style as to that of the younger men like Leonardo or Ghirlandaio. The bust in fact might well be

43

38. Sandro Botticelli · Giuliano de' Medici · Washington

39. Andrea del Verrocchio · Lorenzo de' Medici · Washington

by Verrocchio himself and quite possibly the likeness of Simonetta Vespucci, who was also the *innamorata* of Giuliano de' Medici and whose charms were the subject of no small quantity of Florentine verse. Giuliano's portrait shows the strength and delicacy alike of the style of Botticelli [38], and by and large is the most attractive of several existing variant paintings of the same subject. The little turtle-dove and the broken branch in the foreground are symbolic of mourning for the early demise of his Simonetta. Giuliano's own end came in a spectacular assassination during Mass at the High Altar of the Florentine Cathedral in 1478 in the anti-Medici movement led by the Pazzi family. No untimely death was more widely publicized nor the object of more pathos.

After the Pazzi rebellion, the surviving brother, Lorenzo de' Medici who was given the honorific title of the Magnificent, appears to have ordered a portrait-bust of himself from Verrocchio [39]. It is one of the greatest, most expressively powerful likenesses of the entire Renais-

45

40. LEON BATTISTA ALBERTI
SELF-PORTRAIT · WASHINGTON

sance. Whereas the painted and gilded *Madonna and Child* of terracotta which we have just looked at [36] is by treatment of subject and in spirit part of the continuing current of medieval art in the Quattrocento, the painted terracotta bust of Lorenzo belongs to the very different Age of Macchiavelli's *Prince*. A sketch of the profile by Leonardo (Windsor Castle, Royal Library) shows, in a mirror image like his handwriting, the bust as it was ideated in Verrocchio's *bottega* and hints at the interest that this portrait may have held for Leonardo as a young artist in Florence.[12]

The painted portrait in the formative period of the fifteenth century presented the likeness in profile, or as we have seen in the painted portrait of Giuliano de' Medici, in near-profile. There are a number of reasons for this, but one of the most important is the influence of portrait-medallions cast in metal which, after their revival from Antiquity by the late Middle Ages and particularly by Pisanello in the late 1430s, became the most frequent and most easily diffusable form of portraiture of the Renaissance. The bronze profile plaque [40] of Leon Battista Alberti is far larger than even the most sizeable of the Pisanello examples in medallion-form. It is in fact 'Imperial' in scale and makes one think of incised jewels or cameos with Roman Emperors' portraits in profile. The style is strong, and the piece is not easy to forget once one has seen it.[13]

To the North, in Padua, there was growing up about the same date a young artist who was just as deeply influenced by Roman remains. The small, firmly drawn portrait in profile by Mantegna [41] is a good example of the closeness of the painted portrait of the Early Renaissance to

46

41. ANDREA MANTEGNA · PORTRAIT OF A MAN · WASHINGTON

a sculptural model. Mantegna may be looked on as a kind of sculptor in paint, and indeed may actually have modeled forms, if not actually carved them, in three full-dimensions. His was an art of Stoic invulnerability, imbued with a sense of dignity available to human beings conscious of their place in the continuation of Roman order. Of a later date, and already more fashionable both of mien and dress are the two matched portraits by Ercole Roberti of Giovanni and Ginevra Bentivoglio, the tyrant of Bologna and his wife [43–44]. The sensitive yet firm contour of the profile is placed against the contrast of a dark curtain, which is drawn aside just enough to provide a partial view of the city they control. Here the ease of drawing and above all the charm of color, in which bright hues are enhanced by contrast with rich dark tones, reveal a movement away from Mantegna and the Antique world of marble toward delight in pure painting.

We come now to a more sensational style in North Italian painting. By the early 1480s in Bologna, the moody genius, Niccolò dell'Arca, had begun his great terracotta group, now in S. Maria della Vita, of the *Lamentation Over the Body of Christ*, in which one can almost hear the shrieks and the cries of anguish. In painting, this 'expressionism' was less extreme, though Ercole de Roberti's *Lamentations* may have had influence on Niccolò dell'Arca. The painters were more drawn to the courtly environment of the Dukes or Marquesses at Ferrara and Mantua as well as at Bologna. Thus there arose a unique style of painting which treated 'expressionist' subject-matter in a consciously refined manner, an example in art of what the Romans might have meant with the phrase we have inherited from them of *suaviter in modo, fortiter in re*.

One of the masters of this sophisticated art was Francesco del Cossa, who was born in Ferrara toward 1435 and worked there and in Bologna, where his promising career was closed off by an early death in 1477. His greatest altarpiece was an elaborate compilation of many panels done for a prominent family's chapel in the huge church of S. Petronio in Bologna. The Kress Collection contains no less than three of the panels believed to have come from this altarpiece, in which Cossa's style may be studied to very good effect. The *Saint Lucy* [42], seen at three-quarter length against a gilt background, is a triumphant combination of courtly affectation and of commanding dignity. This saint, according to the *Acta Sanctorum*, lost her eyes in martyrdom. Look carefully, now, at the 'flower' she holds in her left hand.

Cossa's *Crucifixion* [45] is a more masculine interpretation of somewhat the same mood, stressing the superbly strong torso of the Christ not at all unlike Donatello's bronze *Crucifix* in the Santo in near-by Padua which, of course, Cossa could have studied closely and doubtless did. This *Crucifixion* we believe crowned the S. Petronio altarpiece.

The most personal and daring painter of this North Italian group appears to have been Cosimo Tura, born in Ferrara, and who worked there almost exclusively. His style was marked by strongly sculptural masses, animated into twisting yet always controlled movements, almost like the movements of the ballet, dramatized by penetrating effects of light. His influence fell upon the Bolognese Marco Zoppo, who is represented in the Kress Collection by a rare, signed *Madonna and Child* [46] marked by a quiet mood of dignity and an ingenious play of angles and curvilinear rhythms—a kind of combination of Mantegna and Tura. The painting is believed to be the same that, interestingly enough, passed as a Dürer in a Bolognese collection until the signature reappeared, probably as the result of cleaning in the early part of the nineteenth century.

In nearby Ferrara the theme might be similar but in more courtly taste, as for example in Tura's *Madonna and Child in a Garden* [47], in which the gentle beauty of physical type and contemplative mood is played against the angular harshness of the draperies.

The North Italian style of 'painted sculpture' and of 'refined expressionism' found a bridge to fifteenth-century painting in Venice with the art of Carlo Crivelli. His beautiful and large

42. Francesco del Cossa · St. Lucy · Washington

43. ᴇʀᴄᴏʟᴇ Rᴏʙᴇʀᴛɪ · Gɪᴏᴠᴀɴɴɪ II Bᴇɴᴛɪᴠᴏɢʟɪᴏ · Wᴀsʜɪɴɢᴛᴏɴ

44. Ercole Roberti · Ginevra Bentivoglio · Washington

45. FRANCESCO DEL COSSA · THE CRUCIFIXION · WASHINGTON

Virgin and Child [48], from the distinguished Cook Collection in England, presents forms look-ing as if carved from colored rock. The dolphin, symbol of eternal life, is adapted with a remark-ably inventive use of curling scroll-shapes to become the arms of the Virgin's throne. She sits with inward reserve and with a touch of melancholy as she presents her little Son, who shyly looks out upon a rough world which has very little in common with this sophisticated mingling of the artificial and man-made with the natural and the divine.

In Venice, from approximately 1475 to 1500, the fusion of these elements in new brilliance and gentleness of shape and color was the basis of one of the most engaging periods of European Art. As we saw in Florence, the art of sculpture was never completely overshadowed by that of

46. Marco Zoppo · Madonna and Child · Washington

painting. The second half of the fifteenth century in Venetian sculpture was illuminated by a distinguished family of sculptors, the Lombardi, as they were known, from their region of origin. The father, Pietro, developed a serious and powerful mixture of North Italian and some Florentine elements; his sons Antonio and Tullio, particularly the latter, introduced a deeply

53

47. Cosimo Tura · Madonna and Child in a Garden · Washington

48. Carlo Crivelli
Madonna and Child enthroned with Donor
Washington

49. PIETRO LOMBARDO · A SINGING ANGEL · WASHINGTON · TWO VIEWS OF THE STATUE

felt, proto-Romantic, revival of the Antique. Anyone who enjoys the painting of Mantegna or Giovanni Bellini will have no trouble in seeing the quality of contemporary Venetian sculpture, such as the *Singing Angel* [49], which may have been one of a pair holding candelabra for an altar.[14] It is close in pose and mood to Cima's little masterpiece of *St. Helena*. Venetian painting close to the year 1500, as seen in a picture such as this *St. Helena* [50–51], holding her emblem, the True Cross, in a fascinating landscape presents the figure almost as if it were a statue, coming

56

50. CIMA DA CONEGLIANO · ST. HELENA · WASHINGTON

57

51. LANDSCAPE · DETAIL FROM PLATE 50

to life, like Hermione in Shakespeare's *Winter's Tale*. Though the painting is actually of very small dimensions, the figure has a monumental scale that we may find in the largest and most imposing altarpieces of the Quattrocento. The landscape background recalls the world of nature and of men in cities, but illuminated and transfigured under a beneficent sky. The drama of human action as a fulfilling parallel with the divine will is suggested, subtly, by type and attribute.

The artist who made the final reconciliation of these varied elements is the great genius of Venetian painting of the period before 1500, Giovanni Bellini. His was the sensitive touch which could place on a painted panel not only a glimpse of the world as the eye sees it, but as the mind and emotions react to the seasons or even the time of day. The *St. Jerome* [52–53], which is without exception attributed to Bellini by the principal authorities in the field, is perhaps more concerned than is usual in his art with the emphatic treatment of detail at some expense of unity. But the picture projects, as Giovanni Bellini was the first to be able to express it in paint, the feeling of a clear day in June in the Veneto. River, promontory and ruined castle wall, finally, in the deep distance, give way to the view of a pearly island-town rising from the shallow lagoon which stretches out like the promise of summer itself. The chattering of a squirrel breaks for a moment the complete quiet. Then both bird and beast share what peace there is in this world with the Christian version of the Antique philosopher.

52. Giovanni Bellini · St. Jerome Reading · Washington

The *Virgin and Child* [54] is an excellent example of Giovanni Bellini's devotional style of painting. This appears to be the finest of several close variants on one design. The clearly constructed, almost tangible figure of the mother with her Son, shown here nude as if He were a figuration of ancient *Amor*, rises like a pyramid against the sky. Under a soft cloud, reminiscent of early September, is the echoing pyramid of white castle on tawny sunburnt hill, and beyond, the blue light of the heavens fused with the blue haze enveloping the mountains off the Adriatic coast.

60

54. GIOVANNI BELLINI · MADONNA AND CHILD · KANSAS CITY

61

55. CHALICE OF ST. JOHN THE EVANGELIST · REVERSE OF PL. 56

WITH Giovanni Bellini we can see clearly the complete adaptation of a feeling for nature and landscape which was already emerging with the Van Eycks and the Master of Flémalle in North European painting. It appears today that, even though Venice was in close touch through her trade routes with transalpine culture, the Flemish influence was transmitted via the Aragonese Kingdom of Naples and particularly in the person of the Sicilian-Neapolitan, Antonello da Messina, who made a journey to Venice in 1475 and painted there, for the Church of S. Cassiano, a great altarpiece which had almost immediate influence upon Giovanni Bellini and his generation.

The art of the North pursued somewhat different goals in the latter part of the fifteenth and the early part of the sixteenth century from those we have been considering for Italian painters of the last quarter of the fifteenth century. Nevertheless, between Bellini's *Madonna* and the art of the Flemish master Memling, there are points of mood, and even to some extent of color, in common. Memling, as current scholarship confirms, was born in what is now Germany but traveled early to the Low Countries, where he became a leading master in the thriving port of Bruges. His masterpiece is a painted shrine for relics of St. Ursula in the Hospital of St. John in Bruges.

We shall look now at two paintings by Memling in which his attractive way of making images will become very evident. In reality there are three images to be seen. The first picture has both a back and front, an occurrence frequent enough perhaps in the fifteenth century, or even the early sixteenth century, but very rarely to be found in its original state for acquisition in our day. The panel still preserves the image, which was painted originally to decorate its back, somewhat in the same way a medal shows a design both on obverse and reverse. The reverse is a gilt chalice with a snake, set in a stone niche [55]. This is the usual symbol for St. John the Evangelist and possibly points to the man who ordered the painting, more likely a private individual whose given name was John, than the Bruges hospital mentioned above. This kind of composition is one of the earliest manifestations of still-life as a complete and almost independent genre of painting in the North.

The front carries a devotional image of *St. Veronica* holding up the cloth upon which the features of Christ were miraculously imprinted, a kind of metaphor, in saintly legend, of the art of painting itself [56]. The figure of the saint is set in a landscape, one of those views for which Memling became known and which traveled all over Europe. This world of Memling's landscape has been finely characterized as 'ordered and clean' greeting us 'from afar, parklike, estival, with undulating roads... quiet bodies of water, swans, cozy, comfortable houses, blue hills at the horizon—an idyllic homeland where the weather is perpetually summer'.[15] The same exactness of vision of the world about him but sifted and purified by a gentle and optimistic turn of

56. HANS MEMLING · ST. VERONICA · WASHINGTON

thought may be found in the St. Ursula Shrine mentioned above. The *St. Veronica* is painted in somewhat the same marvelously delicate scale and with the same suggestion of other-worldly mystical trance in a setting of remarkably detailed observation of nature.

In contrast to the rather late, or at least middle-period, *St. Veronica*, we have a painting which specialists today believe belongs to Memling's earliest period, when he was just beginning to

come out from the protective cloak of his predecessor Rogier van der Weyden and to assert his own personality. This is the beautiful example of figure-composition in an architectural setting, the *Presentation in the Temple* [57–58]. As has been shown by Erwin Panofsky in connection with other examples, the painter makes use of architectural style to make a statement in his imagery. The 'Temple' in which the ceremony takes places symbolizes the Old Order and as can be easily observed has the rounded arches and figured capitals of the 'old' Romanesque style of architecture. Just beyond with stained glass windows to let in the Light is a choir of 'new' Gothic design which symbolizes the New Order under Grace which the Savior introduces on this earth. Very sensitive portraits of two little girls dressed in almost princely finery in the group of on-lookers are given here also in detail *(see the frontispiece)*. The portraits must be those of daughters of the patron or donor.

Very close to Memling in date was an anonymous painter of the fifteenth century in France who has been called, because of an important work from his hand on the legend of St. Gilles,

58. ENLARGED DETAIL
FROM PLATE 57

59. MASTER OF ST. GILLES · THE CONVERSION OF AN ARIAN BY ST. RÉMY · WASHINGTON

the Master of St. Gilles. He was probably born a Fleming but his career was in France. Two superb panels [59,60], describing incidents from the life of St. Rémy, one the miraculous *Conversion of an Arian* and the other the *Baptism of Clovis*, King of the Franks, belonged to the same altarpiece as the pictures of St. Gilles. This altarpiece on good internal evidence is believed to have been commissioned for the royal abbey of St. Denis just outside of Paris. Appropriately enough for the period the setting for the two scenes shown here are aspects of late fifteenth-century Paris. One shows a remarkably detailed view of the portals of the west front of Notre-Dame on the island of the Cité. The other gives us a view of the entrance to the Royal Chapel

66

60. MASTER OF ST. GILLES · THE BAPTISM OF CLOVIS · WASHINGTON

built by Saint Louis for his palace on the Cité called today the Sainte Chapelle. They may well be the earliest topographical views of Paris made with a trustworthy aim to reproduce accurately what was actually to be seen there.[16]

Another field of activity of Flemish-born as well as French and German artists was late fifteenth-century Spain. The final conquest of the peninsula from the Moors opened not only new territory, but also an era of growing wealth and power. The taste at this time was not Italian so much as Northern. In painting, and to some extent in sculpture also, the 'cry', as Dante might have said, was all for Flanders.

61. MASTER OF THE ST. LUCY LEGEND · MARY, QUEEN OF HEAVEN · WASHINGTON

One of the imports into Spain of some note must have been the large panel, depicting the
Assumption of the Virgin, *Mary, Queen of Heaven* [61–62], by a Fleming called the 'Master of the
St. Lucy Legend'. We may place this painting in time somewhere near the year 1485; it comes
from a convent near Burgos, the capital of Old Castille. The Virgin is shown as being borne
aloft by angels and attended by a choir of heavenly singers and a whole medieval orchestra of
angelic musicians. She leaves an extended landscape below and mounts toward a view of the

68

62. MUSIC-MAKING ANGEL · DETAIL FROM PLATE 61

64. PETRUS CHRISTUS
WIFE OF THE DONOR
WASHINGTON

Court of Heaven, where the Trinity awaits her. The Master of the St. Lucy Legend had both the charm and the occasional disadvantages of the literal-minded. Here the charm is in the ascendant. For it would be a cynic indeed who would not respond to the way in which the artist clothes the miraculous with what he believed would be persuasive reminders of actual experience. The picture is a boon to musicologists who find here not only the proper instruments being played but the correct manner of playing them. Thus the angelic lute-player presents not only a portrait of an instrument but of a player whose fingers are precisely where they should be to sound the note he wishes to play.[17] Even the musical notation on the sheets held by the two singing angels nearest to the Virgin's head has been identified as that accompanying the text of the appropriate hymn, *Ave Regina Caelorum*. The small vocal groups and the relation of stringed to wind instruments is in perfect accord with what is known of actual musical practice of the period, which was dominated by the Flemish *Ars Nova* of Netherlandish composers such as Dufay, Binchois and, later, Josquin des Près. Virtually contemporaneous was the spread of Netherlandish painting style, carried by 1450 right into the heart of the Mediterranean world. Among the chief propagators of Northern influence were the paintings of Petrus Christus of Bruges. Two portraits of donors or patrons [63–64] kneeling in prayer or adoration well illustrate the style of Petrus Christus toward 1460. The gentle characterization of the gentleman and his elegantly dressed wife, the pleasantly realistic details of the clogs discarded on the tiled floor beside the man and the devotional print tacked up on the wall beside the lady, above all the glimpses through a door and a window of calm countryside under the clearest of skies—all these help to explain the popularity of Christus. In addition he must have been reckoned the most faithful follower of the peerless Jan van Eyck. Petrus Christus' paintings were imported very early into Naples along with at least one painting by van Eyck, and the two portraits of the Kress Collection, interestingly enough, came from a collection in Genoa.

Another painting from Spain, this time reportedly from Valladolid, is the *Visitation* [65] attributed to the artist known as the 'Master of the Retable of the Catholic Kings'. This is one of eight known panels from what must have once been a most impressive retable or main altarpiece. The remaining panels are scattered between the Kress Collections throughout the United States as well as the Fogg Museum at Harvard and an unknown owner in Spain. The main altarpieces, or *retablos*, in Spain about 1500 were beginning to take on the uniquely monumental form which they assumed in the sixteenth century. They were, in effect, giant screens with several superimposed rows of large-scale panels arranged around a central composition which was often, especially in the beginning, a sculpture. Thus the *Visitation* must be thought of as part of a series; and the figures which dominate the foreground, pushing out as they do toward the front plane of the panel, should be imagined as being intended to continue the effect of the sculptured design in the central compartment. The artist has taken full advantage, however, of the possibilities of suggesting a deep space on the left side of the *Visitation* where a curving road leads past a moated castle with sweeping landscape of unusual quality. Closer by, the house of Elizabeth and Zachariah is shown being readied by serving girls with mops and ladders for the visit of the Virgin. On the left corner is the coat of arms of the Holy Roman Empire. From this and armorial bearings in other panels of the series it is thought that the *retablo* was originally a royal commission from Queen Isabella to commemorate the marriages of her two children Juan and Joan to Margaret and Philip, children of the Emperor Maximilian. This would place the beginning of the picture series somewhere in the neighborhood of 1493–1495. The place of origin would then be most likely Burgos, the main capital of Castille and the site of one of the most important early schools of painters in Spain.

65. MASTER OF THE RETABLE OF THE REYES CATOLICOS · THE VISITATION · TUCSON

66. Master of the Retable
of the Reyes Catolicos
The Adoration of the Magi
Denver

One of the companion-pieces of the *Visitation* presents the subject of the *Adoration of the Kings* [66]. The theme of adoration brings together a richly ornamented group in the foreground with the very detailed and sharply delineated background of landscape. Rather than of Christus the memory here is of the more angular and expressionist style of Rogier van der Weyden, whose influence we saw a little earlier in the *Presentation* by Memling [57].

Still another and more famous court painter to Isabella of Aragon was the Fleming whose nickname in Spain was Juan de Flandes. He was appointed court painter in 1498 and almost a decade later is believed to have begun the monumental *retablo* for the high altar of San Lazaro in Palencia. Some ten panels have been identified as belonging to this great ensemble, of which four are in the Kress Collection. The *Annunciation* [67] is a much larger picture by actual measurement than appears to be the case. This lightness of scale and soft delicacy of detail is characteristic of Juan de Flandes and is one reason why it is thought that he must have been trained as an illuminator of manuscripts. The light emanating from the Dove of the Holy Spirit above the

67. Juan de Flandes · The Annunciation · Washington

Virgin is an extraordinary study of transparencies. Its circular shape supplies the suggestion of a halo for the Virgin who like the Angel is shown here without a nimbus. This naturalism is given striking scope in the ancient wall with peeling plaster symbolizing the Old Order behind the figures and to the right in the meticulous study of lilies (usually held by the Angel) growing from a bowl of Hispano-Moresque *maiolica*. The shadows from the pot and plant proclaim the existence of a natural light which the supernatural aura around the dove, in a telling bit of symbolism, overcomes.

Thus painting capitalized upon its own inherent advantage over sculpture—the creation of the illusion of light and space, indeed the creation of a 'world' within our world. Sculpture, on the other hand, was able to create a new, freely imagined 'presence' to take a place and carry a meaning in the actual world of nature or of man.

A striking example of the capabilities of both arts toward 1500 may be found in the confrontation of a statue and a painting of one and the same subject: St. Christopher. The name Christopher comes from the Greek, meaning literally the bearer or carrier of Christ and refers to the legend of a Canaanite strong man whose self-imposed duty it was to carry travelers over a dangerous ford in a river. One day he took on his huge shoulders a small child and was astonished that his normally limitless strength very nearly gave out before he reached the other side. The 'child' was revealed as the Christ, who reminded him that it was no wonder that he had found his burden heavy since he had carried Him who in His turn was carrying the sins of the whole world. The theme became popular only late in the medieval period and in the early Renaissance; it may be looked on as a humanized and heroic expression of a thought which had earlier been expressed symbolically by the mystical Lamb of God ('which takest away the sins of the world').

Turn now to the statue [68] which is somewhat over half the size of life and presents the bearded saint in a mantle covering the ordinary day-to-day costume of the Middle Ages. The nobility of the saint and the wonder of the miraculous event, however, shine clearly through. The sculpture is probably French, but from the Northeastern part of France rather than the Southern or Parisian regions. The artist, who was imaginative and original in his solution of the problem of placing the saint in his watery environment in a medium of stone, must have been in touch with Flemish and Rhenish influences.

The painting [69] by the Flemish painter Quentin Massys, measures not even half the height of the statuary group, but it suggests the grandeur of the theme and the gigantic scale of the saint through comparison with rocks, trees and waves in the foreground and, above, the gold-

69. QUENTIN MASSYS · ST. CHRISTOPHER · ALLENTOWN

tinted edges of a bank of delicate clouds. The airy background, which stretches deep back into the space of a harbor, is a striking evocation of very late afternoon or early evening.

Visual imagination was never carried further than by Hieronymus Bosch toward 1500, who originated in the Lowlands close to the Rhine and whose paintings, apparently from an early date, appealed vastly to patrons both in the Netherlands and in Spain. The panel of *Death and the Miser* [70–71] presents a deathbed set in the nave of a church. In the foreground the symbolic armor of the Christian in active life has been abandoned, and a malevolent little hooded demon broods over the cloak thrown down upon the parapet. A charitable but hardly very perceptive friend adds coins to the treasure, to another demon's delight. The door is ajar, and Death with his arrow is about to make his grim appearance on this narrow stage. The drama centers around the Miser, whose emaciated frame is propped up in bed. A fish-faced monster tempts him for the last time with a heavy bag of coins. But there is still hope, for an angel points to a window against which there is a crucifix, whose supernatural light begins to stream downward in a shaft of salvation. Will the dying man see it?

It is characteristic of the irony of the artist that we should be left to savor only the anxiety of the moment of decision. But it is also a tribute to his extraordinary artistic tact that he could join together so much symbolic detail, and so much pantomime of character and gesture, and still preserve clarity of design and a balance of line and color. There is so much in the way of story-telling and semi-humorous touches to distract us from the essential values of composition and form which are the *sine qua non* of the art of painting. And yet rarely was painting put to so trenchant a statement of the spiritual needs of the individual, nor, between the eras of Chaucer and of Daumier, was satire forged into so sharp a weapon for human good.

It is time now to cross, metaphorically, the Rhine and to look at aspects of German painting of the crucial period which encompassed the introduction of Renaissance principles North of the Alps.

70. HIERONYMUS BOSCH
DEATH AND THE MISER
WASHINGTON

71. TREASURE CHEST · DETAIL FROM PLATE 70

79

72. ALBRECHT DÜRER · PORTRAIT OF A CLERGYMAN
WASHINGTON

THERE are three great figures which must capture our interest. The first is Albrecht Dürer, the complex, often self-contradictory, always brilliant and elusive genius—a counterpart in art history to the ever searching, never satisfied figure of Faust. Dürer was born in rather humble circumstances in Nuremberg but as a boy attracted the attention of the Pirckheimer family, whose most famous member, Willibald, is believed to have been the first important link between Dürer and Humanism. Italy as the chief recipient of the heritage of Antiquity must have beckoned insistently to Dürer quite early in his career. His introduction to Italian Humanist art could not very well have been in Nuremberg. But it very likely may have come, with Pirckheimer's encouragement, in the cosmopolitan Humanist center of Basel. In 1495, Dürer made his first journey to Italy, where he must have seen not only Milan and Venice but probably Bologna, Florence and Rome. The assimilation of this experience psychologically was evidently rather lengthy and to all appearances uneven. It seems certain that he found as immediate gains new insights into figure composition and landscape and that perhaps the impressions made on him by the exciting new experience of the world below the Alps were at first more easily translated into landscape than into the human figure.

The problems of proportion and movement in figure drawing and composition, however, were to occupy Dürer's mind over several decades and take up a great part of the pages of his treatise on art called *Die Unterweisung der Messung* (*Analysis of Measured Proportion*, in approximate English translation). He never tired either of the problem of projecting human personality in the art of portraiture. The example chosen for illustration here [72] is a rarity in Dürer's *œuvre* in that it is painted on parchment; it is also one of the very few examples of his portraiture in this country. In its forthright and literal presentation of an individual, modestly set forth against a plain, dark background, it seems to belong North of the Alps, particularly in the quality of the strong, active linear definition of form. The identification of the subject as a 'clergyman' goes back to a very old tradition which linked this portrait with the Lutheran reformer Johann Dorsch of Nuremberg; it has also been suggested as a supposed portrait of the Zurich reformer Ulrich Zwingli.

The *Virgin and Child* [73] has been dated by specialists as very close to Dürer's return to Nuremberg after a two years' stay in Italy. This would place it about 1497, a year or so before the appearance of the celebrated woodcut series of the *Apocalypse*. The group of the Virgin and Child is an interesting adaptation of a motive from Giovanni Bellini. It is beautifully and eloquently drawn. But in its new form it is lacking in Bellini's sure sense of balance and of inward calm. The motive of the window opening on a landscape Dürer appears also to have picked up

73. ALBRECHT DÜRER · MADONNA AND CHILD · WASHINGTON

74. ALBRECHT DÜRER · LOT AND HIS DAUGHTERS · REVERSE OF PLATE 73 · WASHINGTON

75. MATHIS GRÜNEWALD
THE SMALL CRUCIFIXION
WASHINGTON

from his first Italian tour. The true importance of a spacious landscape to him at this time will be found in the composition painted on the reverse of the panel in the scene of Lot and his daughters fleeing the destruction of Sodom [74]. The city is shown as going up in a great explosive burst of flame and smoke while in the deep distance a strangely prophetic mushroom-like feather of smoke proclaims the demise of the sister-city of Gomorrah. These visions of destruction may well have had a connection with nearly universal fears toward 1500 of the coming of the end of the world. One of the woodcuts of Dürer's *Apocalypse* contains a virtual replica of the explosion of Sodom.[18]

Younger than Dürer and much less drawn to the new art of Italy was the painter and engineer Mathis Nithart, called Grünewald. He seems to have been in some ways a more original, apparently more unified, and certainly a more disturbed mind. The emotional power of his imagination was given full scope in the great folding Isenheim altarpiece now in the Unterlinden Museum at Colmar in Alsace. Related to the *Crucifixion* of the Isenheim Altar is the much smaller and earlier variant of the scene, now in Washington [75–77]. Against the dark sky the blood-red robe of the fainting Virgin and the cold opposing color of the robe of the mourning St. John express chromatically the unbearable tensions of the tortured body of the Crucified. The whole world seems about to be shredded and torn into unrecognizable fragments. It is the only painting by

83

76. THE MOURNING MADONNA · DETAIL FROM PLATE 75

Grünewald in this country or indeed, except for the Isenheim altarpiece, outside of Germany. The Kress Collection picture is to be identified with a picture known as the *Small Crucifixion* to differentiate it from the far larger Isenheim *Crucifixion*, and was identified correctly as by Grünewald toward the middle of the seventeenth century. It was engraved in 1605, but until fairly recently (1922) was believed to have been lost or destroyed. Its recovery, particularly after a successful cleaning, has been a major event for scholars and connoisseurs alike. The violence of its 'expressionism' prefigures the principal movement in twentieth-century German painting.

77. ST. JOHN · DETAIL FROM PLATE 75

78. LUCAS CRANACH THE ELDER · MADONNA AND CHILD · TUCSON

The *Madonna and Child* by Dürer's contemporary, Lucas Cranach the Elder [78], carries the
armorial bearings of the Elector of Saxony, considered to be the painter's patron toward 1513
when the picture was executed. The smoothly painted figure, the surface as firm and polished as
the finest enamel, is in its overall design derived from Dürer. The details of pebbled ground,
knotty tree and picturesque castle are characteristic of Cranach's own way of seeing and assem-
bling motives to make a landscape.

Three works lead us now to a consideration of the relationship of the human figure to a landscape setting in the art of the North, both Flanders and Germany, in the early sixteenth century.
The romanticism of Cranach's setting might be compared with the pair of altar wings in mono-
chrome of a small devotional triptych *St. Jerome Penitent* by a Fleming much influenced by Italy,
Jan Gossaert, called Mabuse [79]. The original function of the two panels, which had been
joined together, was discovered during cleaning after they had entered the Kress Collection.
The separation of these two paintings reveals the cinematic quality of their conception as 'still
shots' from a vast panoramic landscape. This landscape, composed of such inherently romantic
elements as rocky outcroppings, Medieval towers, Gothic spires and tree-studded vistas, is made
even more poetic by the illusion of silvery light created by the *grisaille* in which it is painted.

79. Jan Gossaert (Mabuse) · St. Jerome Penitent · Washington

80. PETER VISCHER THE YOUNGER · ORPHEUS AND EURYDICE · WASHINGTON

The legend of the Saint and his emblematic lion is depicted in small scenes throughout the backgrounds of both panels.

The Northern artists appear to us to have had a maximum of originality and freedom in landscape, but they seized eagerly on discoveries in the design of the human figure for the most part made in Italy for adaptation to new groupings and uses. This is seen in the superb plaque by Peter Vischer the Younger which represents the Humanist theme of Orpheus turning back to look at Eurydice [80]. The female nude is derived from Dürer's engraving of the *Temptation*, in turn dependent upon influence from Italy. The boldly drawn Orpheus may owe something to the distant example, transmitted by drawings or even bronze statuettes, of Pollaiuolo. The contrast

88

81. FRANCESCO DI GIORGIO · ST. JEROME · WASHINGTON

with the *St. Jerome in the Desert* attributed to Francesco di Giorgio [81] is instructive even though the Italian relief in its picturesque landscape and multitude of details shows Northern influence. What one feels here is less the drama of the discovery of the nude as a vehicle for artistic expression (see the Vischer relief for this) than the search to find what the Roman poet Lucretius in his *De Rerum Natura* had suggested as a fundamental *datum* of existence: namely, that man was ultimately one with the world of nature. In effect the figure of St. Jerome tends to merge in a subtle way with the landscape setting. This note of 'religious paganism' gives a telling twist to the scene of St. Jerome in the desert and relates it somewhat to the contemplative image of the same subject by Bellini which we looked at earlier.[19]

82. Hans Holbein the Younger · Portrait of a Young Man · Washington

Recent removal of repaints has shown that the *Portrait of a Young Man* [82] should be attributed to the third great German painter of this period, Hans Holbein the Younger. Working in Basel before going to England, Holbein came into contact with Italian art and this picture in its ease and breadth of handling, as much as in its idealistic view of a human being, would appear to be an unusually good example of his style toward 1520.[20] Flatter, more insistent upon

83. MARTIN SCHAFFNER · PORTRAIT OF A LADY OF THE PATRICIAN FAMILY SCHAD VON MITTELBIBERACH · DENVER

84. Pieter Bruegel the Elder · The Temptation of St. Anthony · Washington

detail, whether of fur, brocade, or a ring set firmly on fingers clasped primly, is the *Portrait of a Lady of the Patrician Family Schad von Mittelbiberach* by the German artist, Martin Schaffner [83]. It is remarkable for a search for a kind of absolute visual truth extending to the very fibers of the wood partition of the background. It shows the influence of Holbein but proudly maintains its own individuality.

WE HAVE come in this section of our survey, from Fra Angelico and the Medici in Florence, to a point at which European art began to find both a new general orientation and a more pronounced sense of variety and of regional and personal individuality. True, remnants of the Middle Ages lingered on, if indeed they ever really completely disappeared. Thus, though there is a marvelously developed breadth and grandeur of landscape in the painting of around 1550, given to Pieter Bruegel [84–85], the subject, *The Temptation of St. Anthony*, is full of unexorcized demons. It makes an eloquent plea to forego the 'vanities' of the world and of learning which the Renaissance had attempted to place once again on a sure footing. The blazing church, the ominous birds, the satirical semi-human in a tree trunk with a key to an unknown lock hanging from him, insistently describe a mood of disillusion. Look, however, again at the picture as a whole. It is the landscape, not the figures, which really counts; and to the right the trees and thickets form an irregular avenue into a world which seems fresh and free.

92

85. Trees · Detail from Plate 84

IT is fitting that the last section of this essay should begin with an evocation of the art of the great Venetian innovator 'Maestro Zorzi da Castelfranco', or, as he has been best known since 1548, Giorgione. With his very personal approach to painting in the first decade of the sixteenth century, we seem to come to a watershed in the art's development in Europe. He has been aptly called the 'inventor of the painted lyric' and the 'first single-minded Independent in the history of art'.

It could be said that the fifteenth century in Italy sought to find solutions to the problem of harmonizing figure composition with its pictorial spatial environment from the point of view of an objective observer. The sixteenth century began to modify this formula by bringing both figure and presentation of environment together in such a way as to merge their view with the subjective thought and the emotional tone of the observer's state of mind. *Istoria* no longer controlled. The actors were, so to speak, no longer separated completely from the audience by the apron of a stage. The 'world' of the painting and the psychic fluid 'world' of the individual observer were closer, and at times the barrier between them may have seemed to be removable. Historically speaking, a process of 'seeing' began toward 1500 which ultimately turned the image received through the eye to pure forms and color, entering the conscious mind only to slip beyond into even more mysterious and still deeper reaches of personality. By the mid-nineteenth century the critic Pater could speak of music as the 'condition to which all art aspires'. He likened the unpredictable effect of mood in a painting, as may be recalled in a famous quotation from his essay on Giorgione, to a kind of intimate chord struck by 'an instrument sounded in the twilight as one passes through some unfamiliar room in a chance company'.

The secret of Giorgione's immense reputation seems to have been in his power to suggest that the art of painting was not a public but an intensely private matter; that the aim of painting was not to create the illusion of solids and voids but to charm the individual who looked at it. It must also be said that there is no major figure in the entire history of art, save perhaps Phidias, upon whose extant work there is less assurance of historical fact and where there is more room for disagreement as to what was truly the master's own work as opposed to what was due to his influence.

From a very early date, in fact the year of Giorgione's death, we have evidence that his paintings were much sought after by collectors. Isabella d'Este directed her agent just after Giorgione had died to procure if possible one of two '*Notti*', or Nativity-scenes that were reported to be in private hands in Venice (correspondence of October-November, 1510). Even her great influence was apparently of no avail in persuading the fortunate owner to part with his picture. There has been no decline in prestige nor faltering in demand where Giorgione's paintings have been concerned ever since.

The *Holy Family* [87] has been classified with a small number of pictures, which are gaining increasing scholarly backing as by Giorgione himself. Closely related is *The Adoration of the Shepherds* [86, 88, 89].[21] The two pictures have unusual quality (particularly the latter) and move out well beyond what we have seen in Venetian painting thus far to establish a new mood of revery and to suggest poetically an affirmation in the goodness of the human condition and a quiet, yet vibrant, joy in being alive.

Thus in this painting we move from figure-groups which establish by their form, as much as by their imagery, the unity of succession of the generations between an old man and a new-born infant; through images of humble shepherds who recall the virtues of the pastoral life sung by Horace; to images of a world of perpetual spring—bathed in a golden light and freshened by clear waters. The landscape, which is framed by noble trees and moves to the regular beat of a

94

86. THE SHEPHERDS · DETAIL FROM PLATE 88

87. Giorgione · The Holy Family · Washington

88. GIORGIONE · THE ADORATION OF THE SHEPHERDS · WASHINGTON

89. LANDSCAPE · DETAIL FROM PLATE 88

90. LORENZO LOTTO · A MAIDEN'S DREAM · WASHINGTON

curvilinear rhythm past the tower of a villa on the seashore, contains already the elements of a landscape by Claude le Lorrain.

One immediate effect of Giorgione's example and personal influence is the emergence of a new poetic genre of landscape which modulates, as it were, from Giovanni Bellini's older mode into a new key. With its pastoral setting and overtones of recall of the Golden Age of Antiquity it has been called the Arcadian mode. It is vividly illustrated here by a small, but jewel-like, panel rather romantically called *A Maiden's Dream* [90], by the Venetian artist who came under Bergamesque influence, Lorenzo Lotto. The little picture transposes into painting the quality of the semi-pagan imagery of the great allegorical treatise on mystical love, the *Hypnerotomachia Poliphili*, which was first printed in Venice at the Aldine Press in 1498. It might also serve as illustration to several descriptive passages in the contemporary poem by Sannazzaro, entitled appro-

92. GIOVANNI GIROLAMO SAVOLDO · PORTRAIT OF A KNIGHT · WASHINGTON

priately the *Arcadia*.[22] In one of them the sunset is described as 'gilding the sky' and satyrs at amorous play are characterized, as here, as peeping out behind the protection of tree-trunks. Lotto's development assumed several distinct manners of painting; but he remained intensely personal, and, as the *Portrait of a Man* [91] reveals, he was an acute student of psychology and a master of the extremely difficult task in portraiture of suggesting in the subject a *mind* which seems capable of making contact with the observer's.

Related also to Giorgione was another North Italian who came under Venetian influence. His name was Savoldo, a master of endlessly fascinating effects of light and its reflection from polished surfaces. The *Portrait of a Knight* [92] presents the subject as St. George (one can just make out the fight with the dragon in the distant background). Lights on his armor flicker like cool flames; and the Arcadian element remains, for he carries his broken spear like a shepherd's

93. ROMANINO · THE MYSTIC MARRIAGE OF ST. CATHERINE · MEMPHIS

crook. In the *Mystic Marriage of St. Catherine* [93], by the early sixteenth-century artist nick-named Romanino, this North Italian love of light-reflecting surfaces centers upon the brilliantly painted silken draperies of the Virgin. It is almost as if the draperies alone were intended to carry the general effect of the picture, a device somewhat similar to that later used in the seventeenth century by the Dutch master Terborch. The next painting shows a slightly differing approach in Northern Italy. It is an unusually fine example of the distinguished painter, rare in this country, known as Moretto da Brescia. His power of drawing and solidity of color is to be seen in an impressive *Pietà* [94–95]. Moretto originated, and mainly worked, in the North Italian city of Brescia mid-way between Milan and Venice. The painting style of the mourning Magdalen in particular, has something of the Milanese method of subtle light and shade to create forms in space and yet even more of the sensuous color of the Venetians. Nonetheless the artist retained a very great measure of independence. This painting is a fine example of his power to mingle largeness of conception with pathos and a sense of immediacy with grandeur. Perhaps by way of Bologna he had come into contact with the restraint of Raphael's classicism.

It was the influence of Leonardo da Vinci, however, rather than of Giorgione or Raphael that was felt in the large North Italian center of Milan. Here an idealized 'portrait' of a lady is shown at half-length as *The Magdalen* [96]. It is by Bernardino Luini, probably Leonardo's most distinguished follower from his second Milanese period. The picture is of unusually high quality

102

94. Moretto da Brescia · Pietà · Washington

95. THE MAGDALEN · DETAIL FROM PLATE 94

and translates into a personal Milanese idiom Leonardo's theory of form. The lady's presence emerges mysteriously into our view from dusky shadow, each transition of plane, each volume softly modeled from light to dark so delicately that the shade rests as lightly upon the surface of

96. Bernardino Luini · The Magdalen · Washington

the form as smoke upon a layer of our atmosphere. The idea of a 'smoky' lightness of touch in modeling, is, as we have seen, at least as old as Giotto's immediate tradition on Italian soil. But an enormous distance has been traversed to reach this point in style and expression.

105

97. RAPHAEL (RAFFAELLO SANTI) · BINDO ALTOVITI · WASHINGTON

98. Bindo Altoviti · Detail from Plate 97

The clarity and classic balance of Raphael's painting place it at the opposite pole, as it were, to that of Leonardo and Michelangelo alike. A portrait of a young man [97,98] has been identified by many art historians with the portrait of Bindo Altoviti mentioned by Vasari as having been done by Raphael in Rome after he had absorbed the main rudiments of his style in Perugia and Florence.[23]

We see the image of a blonde youth facing right, but who turns back to look at us. The pose can hardly be said to be 'classic', in the sense in which the usual face-on pose was used so fre-

107

99. IL ROSSO FIORENTINO · PORTRAIT OF A MAN · WASHINGTON

quently in the early sixteenth century. It is more subtle and carried out with remarkable ease. The portrait is a tour de force of composition and very suavely painted. In its firmness of modeling and sureness of drawing in the head and hair it may be related to the aims of Raphael's Roman period, toward 1515–1520. To those aims it adds, however, a strange kind of sensuousness, perhaps a remainder of influence from Leonardo's stay in Rome up to 1515 at the Court of Leo X, perhaps an uncharted aspect of Raphael's personality.

The painted portrait at this period assumed ever-increasing importance, beginning a rise which was to displace somewhat the portrait-bust in sculpture and even the portrait-medal. The rather

100. SALVIATI · BUST PORTRAIT OF A YOUNG MAN · HONOLULU

aggressively composed and boldly painted *Portrait of a Man* by the Florentine, Giovanni Battista di Jacopo, called Il Rosso Fiorentino [99], presents the kind of swaggering yet very complex individual we may meet on the pages of Benvenuto Cellini's autobiography. It belongs approximately to the same date as the portrait which has been identified with Bindo Altoviti and has been described as the only portrait that can be attributed surely to Rosso and is believed, for reasons of style, to have preceded the artist's departure from Florence to work for the royal court in France.[24] A more modest and somewhat later head and shoulders of a bearded nobleman, by the Florentine Francesco Salviati [100], is painted in a fresh and straightforward way. It provides a good example, very characteristic of its time, which may be supposed, from the costume in the Spanish fashion, to be of the Court of the Grand Duke Cosimo de' Medici of the 1540's.

The subtle influence of Leonardo is to be found in the painting of the sixteenth century well outside the direct orbit of his stays in Milan, Rome and Florence. The many-sided movement of the sixteenth century called Mannerism drew in some cases heavily on Leonardo. One excellent

109

101. SODOMA · ST. GEORGE AND THE DRAGON · WASHINGTON

102. Landscape · Detail from Plate 101

example is the exciting *St. George and the Dragon* by the Sienese, Giovanni Bazzi, called Sodoma [101–102]. It has been recognized that the horseman's steed is closely related to a drawing of a horse without a rider on a study-sheet by Leonardo now in Windsor, in the Royal Collection. The monstrous dragon, convulsively coiled back upon itself in a writhing knot of reptilian anguish, is in its origins Leonardesque as well. The background landscape of a hill is, on the other hand, more reminiscent of German landscape, probably through the influence of prints which, by 1520, had already begun to come down over the Alpine Passes into Italy. Such works of graphic art, freely composed and often imbued with a lively Late Gothic fantasy, were a major ingredient of the formation of the Italian Mannerist style. The artist of this picture, however, had not only worked in Leonardo's immediate circle but with Raphael and Peruzzi in Rome. Thus the complexity of the design, so Leonardesque in its mingling of the beautiful, the bizarre and the monstrous, is also a reflection of an unsettled, restless career.

The picture was painted in Siena very probably in 1518. In color and many elements of composition, it recalls vividly the frescoes by Pintoricchio, assisted by the young Raphael and very

103. Bacchiacca · The Gathering of the Manna · Washington

possibly the young Sodoma, of 1503–1508 in the Piccolomini Library of the Duomo in Siena. But where the poetry of the earlier designs was ordered by a sense of architectural scansion, the composition now is best described as an uneasy stretching between polarities: on the one hand the picturesque setting of a romance and on the other the ugly threat of violence and chaos.

An interesting example of Florentine Mannerism is provided by Bacchiacca's *Gathering of Manna* [103, 104], in which sculpturesque figures are mingled together with the maximum of variety. The familiar farmyard animals are juxtaposed to an exotic giraffe. The blue and blue-

104. THE GATHERING OF THE MANNA · DETAIL FROM PLATE 103

green mountains recall the Fleming Patinir, and the organization of the design, whereby small groups of men and women are scattered over most of the panel's surface, is precisely that of Dürer's *Martyrdom of the Ten Thousand*.

What is the meaning of these so frequent borrowings from other artists? Are they symptoms of exhaustion or inferiority, as one used to hear as an explanation? Quite a different answer would be in order now, as our own historical perspective lengthens. Mannerist painting is considered for the most part today as highly inventive, often learned, and most frequently aristocratic. It shunned the obvious. And somewhat on the order of T. S. Eliot's poetry in our own times it rejoiced in creating for the sophisticated viewer echoes of other poetically artistic situations by quotations from styles or compositions. Let us think, then, of such 'borrowings' not as crutches but as evidences of learning and sometimes of wit. Thus in the paintings produced for the courts of Francis I and Henry II in France, under the aegis at first of emigrant Italian artists such as Rosso and Primaticcio, there was also an importation of styles and motives. The

113

signed painting by François Clouet of a great lady in her bath [105–107] contains a reference to Leonardo's nude version of the Gioconda and also, in the deep background with a serving girl, a reference to Titian's composition known as the *Venus of Urbino*.

The subject of Clouet's superbly painted portrait, the finest known of several close variants, is not known. The traditional subject, while the painting was in the Cook Collection in England, was 'Diane de Poitiers', the mistress of the French King, Henry II. The dating of the painting according to current scholarship would be a little late to suit the identification with Diane de Poitiers. Perhaps the allegory refers to a general topic rather than to a specific person. At any event, it should not interfere with our appreciation of the precision of draughtsmanship and almost magically surehanded control of the painting technique. The composition is a striking combination of motives ranging from the unabashed Olympian nudity of the principal figure to the realism of the serving girl in the background and to that of the fruit in the foreground. If the picture is dateable close to 1550, as it seems to be, it antedates by some years the use of fruit in still life which is documented as one of the popular themes of the towering Italian realist of the late sixteenth century, Caravaggio. An Italian painting of still life, done toward 1600 and attributed to Caravaggio, is shown here for comparison [108]. The process that it suggests, of lifting an adjunct such as a plate or basket of fruit out of the context of a larger and more complex design and setting it off as a separate subject is interesting; it may have been in such a way that this familiar type of still life historically won its independence among the European and still later, American *genres*.[25]

106. HEAD OF 'DIANE DE POITIERS' · DETAIL FROM PLATE 105

109. Sebastiano del Piombo · Portrait of a Humanist · Washington

110. STILL LIFE · DETAIL FROM PLATE 109

Another type of still life which has persisted into the twentieth century is the still life of learning or of scholarship. One of the earliest and certainly one of the finest examples known is to be found at the left side of Sebastiano del Piombo's most impressive portrait [109, 110]. The attributes of globe, pen and books, perhaps even an early compass, are those of a scholar-geographer. Sebastiano was a Venetian, a follower of Bellini and Giorgione, and came to Rome in 1511 (presumably soon after Giorgione's death and the closing of his shop in Venice). In

111. PARIS BORDONE · YOUNG HERO ARMED BY BELLONA AND MERCURY · BIRMINGHAM

Rome Sebastiano joined the camp of Michelangelo and opposed Raphael who nevertheless was influenced by him. Except for one visit to Venice just after the Sack of Rome, he remained in Rome as Papal functionary (Keeper of the Seal, or '*piombo*'). Vasari wrote enthusiastically of his ability as a portraitist. The rare example presented here of Sebastiano's portraiture, painted, it is felt in Rome, toward 1520, surpasses even Vasari's praise. Its scale is overwhelming. The power of the dark brooding head and of the Michelangelesque hands is unforgettable.

A similar Roman scale was brought to Venice some years by Titian, influenced by his contact with Jacopo Sansovino the sculptor, Aretino and possibly with Giulio Romano in Mantua.

The unrivalled range of subject-matter which marks Titian's supreme mastery in painting for so many decades in Venice should not obscure his greatness in the various restricted fields or 'genres' of art of his time. One of these fields certainly was portraiture. Where is it possible to find a more varied group of human beings than in the long series of his marvellous portraits? A most attractive picture which reveals Titian's remarkable flexibility in adapting his style to the subject at hand, is the charming portrait of the boy princeling, Ranuccio Farnese [113, 115], of the ruling family of Parma and relative of the Farnese Pope Paul III. Here Titian took obvious pleasure in the subtle tonal structure of the head. The handling of the elaborate sword hilt at the subject's side is an eye-catching bit of virtuosity in paint. One would think that the picture would antedate the more loosely painted Gritti portrait; actually it must be dated nearly a decade later.

The next painting commemorates a great Venetian leader, the Doge Andrea Gritti [114, 116]. Titian's portrait has a tremendous quality of Michelangelesque grandeur and *terribilità*. It is

120

112. Bellona · Detail from Plate 111

painted broadly, almost roughly: the energy and authority of the subject emerges in every smallest detail and brushstroke.

Titian's mythologies and religious paintings are not represented here. But there is an exceedingly rare example, in point of fact the only one outside of Italy, of his decorative ceiling-painting. This is the composition of *St. John the Evangelist on Patmos* [117], originally the central composition of the ceiling of a room in the Scuola, or Confraternity, of San Giovanni Evangelista in Venice. The design is intended to be looked at from below. The strong diagonal leading up from the symbolic eagle at the left carries your eye to the apex of a suggested pyramid where the clouds open to reveal the face of God.[26]

The shadow cast by Titian's fame should not obscure younger contemporaries working in Venice or formed under his influence and working elsewhere. One such painter of great talent and individuality was Paris Bordone, whose signed painting with an allegorical subject-matter *Young Hero Armed by Bellona and Mercury* [111–112] is reproduced here. The principal influence

113. TITIAN (TIZIANO VECELLIO) · RANUCCIO FARNESE · WASHINGTON

114. TITIAN (TIZIANO VECELLIO) · DOGE ANDREA GRITTI · WASHINGTON

123

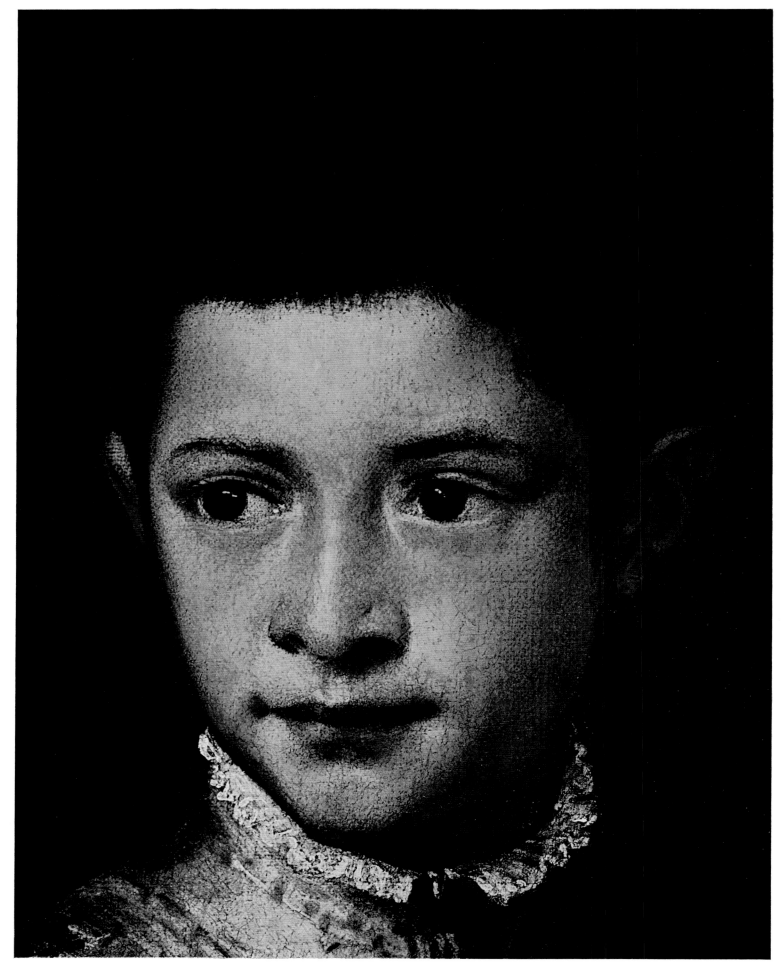

115. Head of Ranuccio Farnese · Detail from Plate 113

116. Head of Doge Andrea Gritti · Detail from Plate 114

117. TITIAN (TIZIANO VECELLIO) · ST. JOHN THE EVANGELIST ON PATMOS · WASHINGTON

on the style is undoubtedly from Titian's early to middle period, let us say up to about 1535. Hence comes the inspiration for the sumptuous color-chord of greens, reds, blues and creamy flesh-tones. Bordone asserts his own sensuous and elegant aims most clearly in the sharp precision of rhythmic figure-composition and in the suggestion of rippling surface-movement as the light caresses the contrasting textures of rich cloth, polished metal and silky hair.

The latter part of the sixteenth century in Venice was as much dependent upon the prestige and example of Titian as was the first part upon Giorgione. Titian himself lived on until 1576, covered with glory and honors and so venerable that there was even then great uncertainty as to his birthdate. The field in Venice was then taken over by two men, principally. One was born in Verona, Paolo Caliari, called Paolo Veronese. Examples of his late period are to be seen in the Kress Collection in Washington. Both are illustrative of two contrasting aspects of his style. The smaller *Annunciation* [118] is light and brilliant in color, alive with a golden illumination. The large *Rebecca at the Well* [119] is a solemn decorative composition in which the figures seem to move slowly and with dignity in a frieze-like scheme against a mysterious and darkened background from which the bulky camels led by Jacob's servant barely emerge to our view. The second great Venetian artist of the period was Jacopo Robusti, called Tintoretto, a painter of unsurpassed vitality and stupendous dramatic power.

126

118. PAOLO VERONESE · THE ANNUNCIATION · WASHINGTON

119. PAOLO VERONESE · REBECCA AT THE WELL · WASHINGTON

120. Jacopo Tintoretto · Doge Alvise Mocenigo and Family before the Madonna and Child · Washington

121. A Boy of the Mocenigo Family as Music-making Angel · Detail from Plate 120

He was also a remarkable portraitist. The large group-portrait chosen here for reproduction is of the Doge Tomaso Mocenigo and his family [120, 121]. It is Tintoretto's challenge to Titian's group portrait of the family of the Doge Andrea Vendramin, painted thirty years earlier, or about 1543. Titian's Vendramin portrait, now in the National Gallery, London, is very close in height to the picture now in the National Gallery in Washington; but Tintoretto's painting is much greater in the dimension of width. It is, in effect, a great mural composition with the glowing figure of the Madonna who has miraculously appeared in the center, and the Doge and his spouse kneeling on either side of the raised dais on which she sits. The standing figure of a Venetian Senator at the left has provisionally been identified as the Doge's brother, Giovanni; the two young men at the right, behind the Doge's wife, as Giovanni's sons, and the two winged boys, masquerading as musician-angels, as his grandsons. An interesting technical detail of this painting is the fact (revealed on examination after cleaning) that the heads of Giovanni and his two sons are each painted on separate pieces of canvas and glued onto the larger canvas. This must mean that these portraits were made in separate sittings. In such a large painting, the studio

130

122. ALESSANDRO VITTORIA · PORTRAIT OF A YOUNG KNIGHT · WASHINGTON

force may well have helped in the draperies and the background, but Tintoretto's direct and vital touch is felt throughout the whole picture, particularly in the heads and the hands. Their freshness and strength of structure is akin to the superbly modeled head of a *Young Knight* by the greatest of the late sixteenth-century Venetian sculptors, Alessandro Vittoria [122]. The bust is almost exactly contemporary with the painting.

In the same period, that is, in the ascendance of Tintoretto, a young Greek from the island of Crete emigrated to Venice, where he eagerly made the most of what he could learn there of Western craftsmanship and style in painting. His name was Domenico Theotocopuli, later to be replaced by a nickname familiar to every student of Western art today: El Greco. The Greek name appears as the first known signature of the artist on a small painting showing Christ driving the money-lenders from the Temple [123]. It was apparently the first of a famous series of versions of the same composition which El Greco continued into his most developed style in Spain. The Italianate forms of his early days in Venice make a striking contrast with the late *Laocoön* [124–126]. Here the distortion of forms for emotional effect, the marvelous sky unified

131

123. EL GRECO · CHRIST CLEANSING THE TEMPLE · WASHINGTON

124. EL GRECO · LAOCOÖN · WASHINGTON

125. VIEW OF TOLEDO · DETAIL FROM PLATE 124

with the figures forecast twentieth-century developments. In this startlingly original vision, based on a Classical theme, El Greco seems to move out of his period to become timeless. The figure at the right foreshadows Picasso's Rose Period, while the pervading quality of hallucinatory power is akin to modern surrealism generally. Yet the picture clearly reveals the period and place in which it was painted. There is still something here of the artist's early stay in Venice, for the nude figure on his back to Laocoön's left (our right) is a clear memory of an invention by Tintoretto; the city against the mountain in the center toward which the Wooden Horse of the *Aeneid* advances is the artist's final home and last resting place, Toledo.

IN SOME RESPECTS El Greco fits the traditional pattern of art in Spain which, since at least the time of the Phoenician traders, welcomed artists from different lands and cultures and transformed what they brought with them as technical and spiritual baggage to a new power of intensity. El Greco on the other hand is not readily classifiable either as to nationality or as to broad concepts of period-style. Can one truly say that he was a Mannerist, or, except by stretching the term, that he belonged to the Baroque? It is probably symptomatic of great changes in European culture toward 1600 that simple stylistic categories do not function very well as handy

126. STANDING NUDES · DETAIL FROM PLATE 124

pigeon-holes for our later understanding of what occurred in the two hundred and fifty years between the opening of the seventeenth century and 1850. It appears as if we were likely to gain a better view if we proceed by looking for continuing groundswells of attitudes and of sensibility beneath the surface movement of historical change and to give full value to the personal contributions of individual artists, in all the variety of their training and aims.

What is found toward 1600 is a growing community of general ideas about art over all of Europe with an accompanying emphasis upon the individual artist's right to assert his own

136

128. Tanzio da Varallo
St. John the Baptist in the Wilderness
Tulsa

genius. Perhaps at no time in the history of Western painting were the opportunities broader and more beckoning. The year 1600 opened upon a movement which was certainly realist and also upon a movement which we should call classicist. The next years were to see what might be termed forthright visual reporting, they were also to witness emotional interpretations which might approach effects of the theatrical or of the operatic.

Let us begin with the Neapolitan area, where, under a Spanish Viceroy, the cultural ties with Spain were strong. The very fine, large-scale altarpiece by Massimo Stanzione, *The Assumption of the Virgin* [127], provides a vivid impression of the realism mingled with piety and drama which was shared by the Schools of Valencia and Naples towards 1630. Here we are led in easily to a space which holds a drama performed by people who seem to be real. Even the Virgin surrounded by athletic little *putti* appears to have been painted from a model. Among the men others seem even closer to a natural and unvarnished truth.

A large part of the striking shift in vision which brought the normal, banal and even ugly aspects of the world into the realm of emotion and of art was due to the daring example and courage of the painter Michelangelo Merisi, whom we know from his birthplace in North Italy as Caravaggio. Before he started on his rebellious career and restless travels, which were to end

137

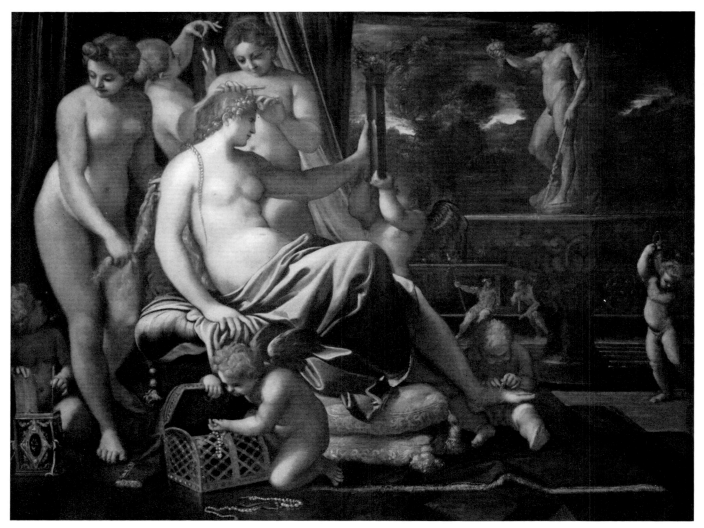

129. ANNIBALE CARRACCI · VENUS ADORNED BY THE GRACES · WASHINGTON

all too soon and too unhappily with his death in 1609, Caravaggio had worked for a time in and about Milan. A most interesting echo of this early period of his is the *St. John the Baptist in the Wilderness* by the Lombard, Tanzio da Varallo [128]. The dramatic presentation of the subject is enhanced by a remarkable romantically wild landscape of wooded mountain scenery at the left. The effect of dramatic contrast of light and shade and the feeling of the observer that he actually is close enough to share the space of the picture with the subject came doubtless from Caravaggio.

Another aspect of the seventeenth century is best seen in the work of Annibale Carracci, one of three painters who were close relatives. Born in Bologna, and active himself after 1595 in Rome, Annibale Carracci sought to build a foundation for the art of his time by assimilating the best of what he could study of the sixteenth-century masters. His transformation of the tradition was subtle and complete. It was not superficial, for in studying and using Raphael, Michelangelo and Titian he found ways to rejoin the great continuing classic stream of Western art which had at one time or another in their careers caught them up. *Venus Adorned by the Graces* [129] combines the Venetian mode with echoes of Raphael's Roman period. Under the elaboration of detail and rays of flickering light is a substructure of calm and enduring forms. It consists of large rhythms of gesture, pose and movement reminiscent of the easy grace and authority of the great sculptors of Antiquity. The principal figure in fact appears to be derived from the Antique statue of the *Nile* moved by Michelangelo to the Campidoglio in Rome toward the middle of the sixteenth century. This reaffirmation of the classic ideal may be compared with

130. NICOLAS POUSSIN · THE HOLY FAMILY ON THE STEPS · WASHINGTON

Poussin's triumphant manner of the middle of the seventeenth century. *The Holy Family on the Steps* [130] looks to Raphael and perhaps also to Andrea del Sarto. But the total composition in its extraordinary sense of balance between mass and void, light and shadow, humanity and architecture, freedom and order, belongs entirely to Poussin's own classic genius. He was, as is well known, a Frenchman whose Latinity could find a compatible environment only in Rome.

The Kress Collection *Holy Family on the Steps* was painted in Rome at the peak of Poussin's powers toward 1648, and reveals admirably the careful interplay of naturalistic imagery and abstract form which marks his painting at its very best. The figures are grouped, with the lovely Virgin at the center, in an ordered, pyramidal scheme—very much, actually, like the composition of sculpture in the triangle-shaped pediment of an Antique temple. The precisely shaped stone forms of an idealized architecture, also based on the remains of Antiquity, provide a harmonious environment. Behind the darkened profile of Saint Joseph, who is shown here as a geometer or mathematical philosopher, a second flight of steps continues to the suggestion of a high, broad platform. This we feel, but cannot see, as a climax of pure space and intellect—an imagined acropolis. Beyond it, as in Raphael's architecture of the *School of Athens* in the Vatican, there is only the clear ether of the heavens and the purity of a light-filled cloud.

Poussin's art was not an escape from reality but a presentation of a 'super-reality'. Based on Nature and the world of men and ordinary things, this ideal of art was aimed at the creation of a higher, more 'beautiful nature'. The talent of Orazio Gentileschi, born in Pisa and trained in Florence, presents a more intimate, yet no less 'real' approach. His striking *Portrait of a Young*

139

131. ORAZIO GENTILESCHI · PORTRAIT OF A YOUNG WOMAN · HOUSTON

Woman [131] must be a study from life of a young model placed very much in the same pose as that we saw earlier used in the 'Bindo Altoviti', for a subject which would later be worked up into a more formal composition, probably of a Sibyl. The sensation of closeness of the subject to us, the delicacy of the play of light and shade, the variety of textures—all modify a kind of

132. SIMON VOUET · THE MUSES URANIA AND CALLIOPE · WASHINGTON

Tuscan classicism toward a broader and more human expression. Gentileschi worked in Rome and in North Italy and spent the latter part of his career in England.

A second comparison with Poussin might very appropriately concentrate for a moment on the art of his rival, Simon Vouet. Vouet painted a few portraits and some fine religious altar-pieces. But his favorite subject-matter was an elegant kind of mythology and allegory adapted from classical sources, which formed the basis for the decoration of ceilings and galleries in royal, princely or noble houses in France.

Vouet's court-style is illustrated here [132] by *The Muses Urania and Calliope* seated at the base of a Roman ruin in a gently rolling landscape and attended by wreath-bearing Italian *amorini* who have to all appearances well begun the transition to French *amours*.[27] The clear, fully-rounded shapes of the figures are not so much broken up by intricate effects of light and shade as in the classicism of Poussin or of his Italian forerunner Annibale Carracci. Instead outlines are kept unbroken and foreground and deep distance carefully differentiated. This style is clearer, more logical, if anything, more 'classic' in the French sense than anything we have seen up to this point.

The contrast with Vouet's youthful manner when he was in Italy is remarkable. In his travels and sojourns in the various Italian centers, the young Frenchman was attracted to a fairly wide gamut of styles, none more powerful as a magnet than Caravaggio's as he could study it in paintings in Rome.

An example of the influence of Caravaggio is to be seen in the painting *St. Jerome and the Angel* [133]. This has been ascribed on a stylistic basis to Vouet, who went to Italy in 1612 and

133. SIMON VOUET · ST. JEROME AND THE ANGEL · WASHINGTON

worked there, principally in Rome, before returning to France where he became court painter
under Louis XIII. The presence of the models comes through insistently; but the magical quality
of the brushwork transforms what might have seemed a literal view into a compelling artistic
vision. The delicate yet logical effects of the light alone make of this picture a telling example of
the double quality that the seventeenth-century emulator of Vasari, Filippo Baldinucci, praised
in his *Life* of Bernini, as the 'sensitive and the true'.

As the seventeenth century continued from decade to decade it produced painting of greater
and greater variety. The solemn, hard realism of the Spaniard Zurbaran is well illustrated by the
severely ordered painting [134] done probably for a Jeronymite establishment in Seville toward
1640. To the left St. Paula is seated with her daughter, St. Eustochium. Fifth-century followers
of St. Jerome, they were the founders of his Order and are shown here in an idealized reconstruction of their appearance in what was then 'modern dress'.

If Vouet's painting of the saint has the precision and subtlety of the French seventeenth century, Zurbaran's St. Jerome has an implacable quality of unyielding truth that was a part of the
Spain of Cervantes. The light and dark alternating in the pattern of the monastic habits is carried dramatically into the background. Against the sharp edge of the curtain that cuts the picture
virtually in half is outlined not only the sculpturesque head of the bearded saint but, in the
exact center of the design, his gesturing hand—the more eloquent for the uncompromising
representation of the bony knuckles and the wrinkles of old age and as a symbol of a harsh,
ascetic ideal.

142

134. Francisco de Zurbaran · St. Jerome with St. Paula and St. Eustochium · Washington

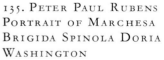

135. Peter Paul Rubens
Portrait of Marchesa
Brigida Spinola Doria
Washington

In Flanders by 1625 curvilinear rhythmic patterns became a generally practised method of design. Into a pictorial environment of full, rich forms warm with the ripeness and exuberance of life might be introduced motives taken from Italianate sources. The journey to Italy was taken by the Fleming Rubens early in his career and by his pupil Van Dyck also. Rubens spent years working in Mantua and in Genoa, whence came the splendid portrait, originally a full-length, of the *Marchesa Brigida Spinola Doria* [135, 136]. The exactness of observed detail and the tightness of manner are characteristic of this period of Rubens' early development.

136. HEAD OF MARCHESA BRIGIDA SPINOLA DORIA · DETAIL FROM PLATE 135

137. Peter Paul Rubens · The Last Supper · Seattle

Later, when he returned to Flanders, he became the head of a vast organization of assistants and pupils which has been well described as a picture-factory. This is one reason for the importance and great artistic value of the sketches which the master did himself at small scale before giving them to be enlarged by his assistants. The freedom and vivacity, both of brush and color, of a sketch by Rubens may be a revelation.

Two of such sketches reveal his mastery not only of fluent oil-technique but of composition in a restricted space (for a specific emplacement) of a complex group of figures. The first of these, for a ceiling decoration, is a striking parallel to the other. It is the *Last Supper* [137]. The moment chosen by the painter is Christ's announcement of His coming betrayal and expected death.

146

The second sketch makes use of the Roman *adlocutio* or general's speech to his troops as the basis of design [138]. The subject *Decius Mus Addressing the Legions* concerns a Roman consul who received in a dream the intelligence that on the morrow's battle either the leader or his army would be destroyed. In order to save the Legions, he chose to die himself.

In both pictures it is worth noting that Rubens has reduced to a minimum the number of figures. He suggests a whole Legion with but five standard-bearers and a Church with only one complete figure and the suggestion, often the barest, of half a dozen more. He sets the protagonist of each tragic situation somewhat apart and at the same time brings that figure, by his all-over pattern of light and color, into the unity of each design.

139. Anthony van Dyck · Queen Henrietta Maria with her Dwarf · Washington

This was one side of Rubens' genius. The other, more elegant, was taken up by Anthony van Dyck, whose graceful path led from success as a young painter in Genoa to even greater triumphs in Antwerp and in England. The portrait of *Queen Henrietta Maria*, wife of Charles I, with her dwarf, Jeffrey Hudson, and her pet monkey 'Pug' [139, 140] is now recognized as the first and finer of two versions. It was probably painted in 1633; its composition of the great lady standing by a column and a grand curtain of falling drapery became a guide-post for Gainsborough in the next century.

141. PHILIPPE DE CHAMPAGNE · OMER TALON · WASHINGTON

WE COME now to still another aspect of seventeenth-century painting. This might be called Realist, but its aims and achievements must be admitted to be a great deal more than a transcription of reality. There is a grandeur and sumptuousness in the portrait of 1645 of the Parisian Jurist, *Omer Talon*, by Philippe de Champagne [141, 142] that is worthy of a royal portrait. The style is uncompromising in every detail: from the chipped stone of the pavement to the time of day marked by the meticulously rendered clock standing beside a pen, a book and the subject's finely drawn and painted hand. Two discordant reds harmonized by black, white and grey form its startling and bold color combination. It is a superb psychological study of an intelligent and not untroubled man.

150

142. STILL LIFE · DETAIL FROM PLATE 141

143. Gian Lorenzo Bernini · Monsignor Francesco Barberini · Washington

144. MONSIGNOR FRANCESCO BARBERINI · DETAIL FROM PLATE 143

This painting should be looked at in sequence with two other works in the Kress Collection. The first is the masterly posthumous portrait of *Monsignor Francesco Barberini* [143, 144] by Gian Lorenzo Bernini made about 1625. It is in the style of Bernini's early period at its maximum development, toward its close in fact. This bust contains one of the rare and difficult *pentimenti* (alterations of composition) to be found in sculpture. Skillfully inserted into the tip of the beard is a triangular piece of marble so carefully carved to fit into the design that the addition is almost invisible. Apparently the artist, having carved the prelate's beard with a triangular division in the center, was dissatisfied with a composition which repeated the same form in three consecutive positions: the beard, the points of the collar, and the opening of the cape; he therefore altered the shape of the beard to improve the composition. There is in it much the same approach to nature and the same emphasis on mastery of touch and technique that may be found

153

145. LOUIS LE NAIN · A FRENCH INTERIOR · WASHINGTON

in the head of St. Jerome attributed to Vouet's Roman period [133]. There is the same feeling for structure veiled by delicacy and of dignity enhanced by subtlety. A more humble view of French life is to be found in the art of the Le Nain brothers, particularly Louis Le Nain, to whom are normally attributed scenes of peasant life such as that in a fine picture called *A French Interior* [145]. The interest in still-life detracts no more than in Philippe de Champagne's portrait of Talon [141] from the human qualities and values of the sitters, who here seem hardly posed at all.

It would be logical to look to the Lowlands for the most complete repertory of realism, for not only was there a tradition, dating from the Middle Ages, of naturalism in the background, but in the seventeenth century a sturdy middle-class culture to patronize such an art. The intimate and quiet side of Dutch life is the subject of the small, detailed painting by De Hooch called *The Young Mother* [146]. Here all the prosaic paraphernalia of a middle-class interior are given a touch of poetic value by the sensitive handling of effects of light in which De Hooch was second only to his one-time rival in Delft, Vermeer. One could compare this for a moment with

154

146. Pieter de Hooch · Young Mother · San Francisco

147. BERNARDO STROZZI · ST. LAWRENCE GIVING THE TREASURES OF THE CHURCH TO THE POOR · PORTLAND

a powerful and dramatic painting by the Genoese Bernardo Strozzi [147, 148], who worked for a time in Venice. The subject is one which Strozzi painted several times: *St. Lawrence giving the Treasures of the Church to the Poor*. The Kress painting has been judged the last and most developed of the known versions. The censer which is the focal point of interest in the composition is a remarkable piece of *bravura* in oil paint. Here influences from Flanders which Strozzi found in his native Genoa in the art of the young van Dyck make their presence felt and bring us once again to the realization of the extent of interchange and unity in seventeenth-century European painting.

European painting, both in Italy and in the North, made some of its most spectacular strides in landscape. While Claude, in Italy, following upon Giorgione, Annibale Carracci and the Antique evolved a type of ideal landscape, the Dutch painters developed to a remarkable extent the possibility of representing actual scenery and views of actual places in art. Among all Dutch topographical paintings, which are portraits of places rather than landscapes, one of the most interesting is the view of *Santa Maria della Febbre*, with its obelisk on the site of the Circus of Nero, next to St. Peter's then still under construction in Rome [149]. This small picture by Pieter Saenredam was not painted on the spot, for the artist never left the Lowlands. It was done from

148. A Censer · Detail from Plate 147

149. Pieter Jansz. Saenredam · The Church of Santa Maria della Febbre, Rome · Washington

a drawing by the earlier Dutch artist Martin van Heemskerk, made toward 1530. Saenredam, whose dryly unpretentious and straightforward style has a great appeal for twentieth-century eyes, is known to have had some of Heemskerk's drawings in his possession. This painting then is, again, something much more than the transcription of reality. It is an effort to recapture a moment of the past in a distant place. This may be a suggestion in very simple terms of the following century's double urge toward Historicism and Romanticism.

It would be quite wrong, however, to confuse the directness of Saenredam's approach with the infinitely more complicated and imaginative approach of eighteenth-century artists, whether in Italy or in France. An excellent example of the contrast would be to look at the evocation of Rome and its monuments in the painting of 1723–1729 entitled *Memorial to Admiral Sir Clowdisley Shovell* [150, 151]. The picture was commissioned in Italy as one of a series of twenty-four allegorical compositions celebrating famous Englishmen, then alive or recently dead. The artists of the Shovell painting were the Venetians Marco and Sebastiano Ricci. To Marco, the younger and more clearly eighteenth-century man, went the opportunity of creating the surprising monument and the even more extravagant and theatrical scenery of ruined temples, pyramids and statuary. To his uncle, Sebastiano, went the figures. They are full of life and very engagingly painted. To the left front, a young man, perhaps an Englishman on the Grand Tour, is absorbed in sketching. To the center stands an exotic Moor in a turban, a visual reminder that a large part of the admiral's claim to fame was from operations off the Barbary Coast as well as the capture of Gibraltar.

The Italian eighteenth century in painting has been well known, but far from completely except to specialists. Recently attention has been focused on some of the less familiar men to bring them back into the view of general public knowledge. From this inquiry there are emerging a number of attractive painters of apparently lasting significance. One of these is the Neapolitan

150. Sebastiano and Marco Ricci · Memorial to Admiral Sir Clowdisley Shovell · Washington

151. MOOR AND NEGRO · DETAIL FROM PLATE 150

Gaspare Traversi, whose semi-serious, semi-humorous canvas from a series on the arts is entitled *Music* [152]. Its subject is presented as an eighteenth-century *salon* version of Susanna and the Elders. Another is Giacomo Ceruti, a Lombard who worked as well in Venice. Ceruti was a fine portraitist in a realistic vein, and to him also have been attributed a number of scenes of everyday life. Some are of aristocratic functions in Venetian palace drawing rooms. Others, such as *The Card Game* [153], seem to recreate in an Italian idiom seventeenth-century tavern scenes by Teniers or van Ostade. Somewhat in the same way and toward the same time, the young Greuze made use of the same painters for a like purpose in France.

More original and more given to flights of fantasy was the Genoese Alessandro Magnasco. His figure-compositions revolved around two themes: satires of monasticism and of humanity in general under the characters of the Italian *Commedia dell' Arte*. A canvas depicting *Pulcinella Singing with his Many Children* [154] is a good example of Magnasco's brilliant style in this manner. More serious and actually a landscape with figures is the *Baptism of Christ* [155, 157]. This has recently been cleaned, and the emergence of brilliant nuances of blues, greens and pinkish reds has been a revelation of the range of Magnasco's color. The freedom of brushwork in which the whole area of the canvas comes alive in sparkling slashes and little rivulets of light is both daring and, here, unusually successful in effect.

153. Giacomo Ceruti · The Card Game · Raleigh

154. Alessandro Magnasco · Pulcinella singing with his many Children and a Lute-Player · Columbia

155. ALESSANDRO MAGNASCO · THE BAPTISM OF CHRIST · WASHINGTON

Against the experimental turn of mind of Magnasco, who in a way took some elements of Tintoretto's style and pushed them to an extreme, there should be placed the more conservative figure-painters. One, Sebastiano Ricci, we have met recently in connection with the memorial composition to Sir Clowdisley Shovell. In a *Battle of Centaurs and Lapiths* from his hand [156], the violent athleticism in the foreground is wittily set off by the struggling figures in the background—white as marble statuary under the moonlight. In Bologna, the slightly younger Donato Creti was a master also of violent action. According to eighteenth-century criticism his masterpiece was the picture reproduced in this volume called *The Quarrel* [158]. The subject is the quarrel which occurred between Philip of Macedon and his son Alexander, later to be known as Alexander the Great, at the wedding feast of Philip and his second wife. It is believed to have had special meaning for the artist, who was reported to have been driven from home by a threat from his father. In comparison to late sixteenth-century painting (Veronese), which the picture most resembles, the figure-style is not only more active but less impressive in scale. What is gained is an unusually successful impression of space in depth, obtained tonally as well as by perspective.

156. SEBASTIANO RICCI · THE BATTLE OF THE CENTAURS AND LAPITHS · ATLANTA

The painter Giovanni Battista Piazzetta stood between the schools of Bologna and of Venice in the mid-eighteenth century. An avid student of realistic appearances, Piazzetta displayed originality and unusual power and monumentality as a composer of figures. His decorative canvas, *Elijah Taken Up in the Chariot of Fire* [159], is a striking achievement; it is the only painting of such size and scope in this country which can give a fair idea of the artist's potential. The compositions of Giovanni Battista Tiepolo are much more common in America. He too was a great decorator on a grand scale. The painting reproduced here [160], however, reveals him in a more personal and less grandiloquent mood. The subject, *Apollo Pursuing Daphne*, retains the element of action in the pursuit. But the marvelously beautiful figure of the nymph, as she is changed into a laurel tree, is reminiscent of the poses used by the Renaissance masters. The memory of Titian certainly is not completely absent here.

The most original contribution of Venetian eighteenth-century art was perhaps in topographic painting. The chief artists were Antonio Canale, called Canaletto, his nephew and follower Bernardo Bellotto, and Francesco Guardi. The view called *The Portello and the Brenta Canal at Padua* [161, 162] is among the finest things of this kind that Canaletto ever produced.

157. CHRIST AND ST. JOHN · DETAIL FROM PLATE 155

158. DONATO CRETI · THE QUARREL · WASHINGTON

159. Giovanni Battista Piazzetta · Elijah taken up in a Chariot of Fire · Washington

168

160. GIOVANNI BATTISTA TIEPOLO · APOLLO PURSUING DAPHNE · WASHINGTON

161. Antonio Canaletto · The Portello and the Brenta Canal at Padua · Washington

162. The Brenta Canal · Detail from Plate 161

163. Francesco Guardi · Campo San Zanipolo · Washington

It is dateable about 1735 or 1740 and was the product of many studies which show that the artist worked from slightly differing angles. It is extraordinary how much detailed observation has been packed into the painting. Yet its over-all effect is strikingly clear and uncluttered. The contrast in manner with Francesco Guardi's much smaller *Campo San Zanipolo* [163, 164] is evident, but the method of design is not too different. Guardi moves away in order to give room for his little figures, each made up of only the fewest possible deft touches of paint. His is the ultimate magic, for one forgets the drawing, even the ostensible subject, in order to enjoy the flicker of light and the flecks of color as exciting occurrences in themselves.

Recent scholarship has fully confirmed the tradition that Guardi in his early period was a follower of Antonio Canaletto in his panoramic view-painting. Canaletto's discoveries were carried out more faithfully by his talented nephew, Bernardo Bellotto. Although he achieved his

164. CHURCH OF SS. GIOVANNI E PAOLO · DETAIL FROM PLATE 163

165. Bernardo Bellotto · Entrance to a Palace · El Paso

reputation on his home-ground of Venice and the mainland near Padua, Dolo for example, Bellotto travelled far afield. He worked in Vienna, in London, and last of all in the Polish capital of Warsaw, from 1767 until his death in 1780. The painting reproduced, *Entrance to a Palace* [165], is from this last period in Warsaw. It belongs to a fairly large group of palace projects, elaborate conceptions which circumstance never permitted him to realize. An interesting detail here is the fountain in the court which has Bernini's *Apollo and Daphne* imaginatively placed upon it. In the foreground the figures standing on the left have been recently identified as members of the Potocki family. Doubtless it was they who commissioned this painting.[28]

French eighteenth-century art developed out of the last years of the Court of Louis XIV where artists such as the painter La Fosse and the sculptor Coysevox gave a new direction to the heavy and rather pompous 'Louis Quatorze' style. As the 'Sun King' grew older, the young ideas of the new generation naturally came into view; it is to the old king's credit that he encouraged these developments.

The name of Antoine Watteau is the one to conjure with in this period of freshness and change. Born in the town of Valenciennes, which belonged as much to the Lowlands as to France, he came early under Flemish influence, particularly that of Rubens. Once in Paris, he did not join the court artists but instead worked for wealthy individuals, among them the banker Crozat, who gave him the hospitality of his home and allowed him to study his extraordinary collection of paintings and drawings. The composition of *Ceres* [166], the only survivor of a series of four seasons painted by Watteau toward 1712 for Crozat's dining room, is shown here. The figure, attended by the symbolic attributes of Summer, the zodiacal signs of the Lion and the Crab (here a crayfish), is throned in easy grace upon a cloud and a sheaf of wheat. The influence of Rubens is moderated, but its warmth is still felt. The process of a change toward the delicacy and prettiness of youth, as opposed to its exuberant vitality, is to be seen in the charming attendants to the right.

Much the same kind of change, to longer proportions, more graceful attitudes, more delicacy in detail, is to be seen in the rather recently rediscovered *Morceau de Reception* of 1701 by the French sculptor, Robert le Lorrain, *Galatea* [167, 168]. The piece, like some late seventeenth-century 'reception pieces' carved as proof of competence to become a member of the Academy in Paris of painters and sculptors, is small in scale. It is a fanciful adaptation of the Antique with gentle overtones of the Roman Baroque, as in the dolphins swimming at the figure's feet.

The new style was evident also in portraiture in sculpture. The major figure in the carry-over into the eighteenth century was Antoine Coysevox, for two decades previously a member of the 'team' of artists who had worked under the King's master-foreman Le Brun to populate both the Château and the Park at Versailles with figures in marble, bronze, and stucco. The combination of dignity of position, individuality of person and lightness of touch in execution was no easy matter to achieve. And yet these are the qualities one should look for in the style of a portrait-bust of the late period of Louis XIV. The one shown here [169] is by Coysevox and represents *Louis of France*, the *Grand Dauphin*, close to the year 1700.

With painting and sculpture alike, art in eighteenth-century France took a well defined course which can be followed in a series of outstanding examples in the Kress collection.

Watteau died early; the heritage of his art passed to two painters in particular. The first, Jean-Baptiste Pater, of Watteau's own generation, was best known for his figure compositions of fashionable ladies and their amorous admirers in the setting of a park, known as *Fêtes Galantes*. In this genre, which Watteau seems to have started, memories of Rubens and Giorgione were fused in the subtlest possible way with the gracefully erotic tendencies of the French Regency.

166. Antoine Watteau · Ceres · Washington

176

167. Robert le Lorrain · Galatea · Washington

168. HEAD OF GALATEA · DETAIL FROM PLATE 167

169. ANTOINE COYSEVOX · LOUIS OF FRANCE, THE GRAND DAUPHIN · WASHINGTON

170. JEAN-BAPTISTE-JOSEPH PATER · FÊTE CHAMPÊTRE · WASHINGTON

Such paintings recreate a new kind of Arcadia. Seldom did such attractive ladies receive more daintily attentive homage. The spirit of these little figures is that of Watteau's *Ceres* extended to a stage. It is interesting to compare Pater's *Fête Champêtre* [170, 171] with the painting by his slightly younger contemporary, Lancret, called the *Picnic after the Hunt* [172, 173]. This painting, like Pater's, is small, not for easy handling, but to fit appropriately into the much reduced scale of interior spaces and their elaborate decoration so characteristic of the Regency period. Lancret's painting belonged to the greatest collection of his work, made by Frederick II, the Great, of Prussia. It is noticeably more 'modern', more realistic than Pater's idealized fantasy. The setting is related to a landscape of human living. The dogs are accurately portrayed. The lady and the gentleman beside her, as the painting's focus, seem less separated from the conventions and activity of actual life than Pater's.

The artist above all who pursued the possibilities of an art closer to bourgeois life was the Parisian painter, Jean-Baptiste-Siméon Chardin. He was unquestionably influenced by the 'Little Dutch Masters', such as De Hooch. But his feelings for form and the quality of material things as well as human beings seemed to move on to a different, and higher, plane. The *Kitchen Maid* [174], one of two figure-pieces by Chardin in the Kress Collection, was painted in 1738 and was bought by Prince Liechtenstein, the Austrian Ambassador to France, in Paris after it had been shown in the *Salon* of the Academy.

171. GROUP OF FIGURES · DETAIL FROM PLATE 170

172. Nicolas Lancret · Picnic after the Hunt · Washington

182

183

173. HOUNDS · DETAIL FROM PLATE 172

174. Jean-Baptiste-Siméon Chardin · The Kitchen Maid · Washington

Seemingly without effort a number of carefully studied motives of apparently the most obvious and banal nature (a tired young scullery-maid, a bowl of eggs, a pile of turnips, a butcher's
block with a cleaver) are put together into a moving relationship. The whole has beauty and
meaning. Richness is imparted not so much by imagery or brightness of hue, as by the texture
of the paint itself. This feeling for paint-texture, together with the effect of complete stillness
which suggests a subtle chord of harmony between the human and the inanimate, prefigure
Cézanne's early still-lifes and portraits of more than a century later. Though nothing is 'hap-
pening', one feels the painting is not concerned with a pose or an attitude. The pause of weari-
ness and boredom is felt as part of an *action* which has begun and we feel must inevitably con-

175. JEAN-MARC NATTIER
JOSEPH BONNIER DE LA MOSSON
WASHINGTON

tinue. Judging from his writings, the French philosopher-critic Diderot must have pondered the message of this painting, whose modesty of scale bears so little relation to its intrinsic greatness. He once wrote: 'An attitude is one thing, and an action is another thing. Every attitude is false and little; every action is beautiful and true.'[29] While these words apply very aptly to France in the second half of the eighteenth century, they have a deeper echo. It is almost as if one were hearing a remark of the Master preserved by a confidant of Michelangelo's or of Alberti's.

Dated 1745 is the portrait by Jean-Marc Nattier of the dilettante scientist *Joseph Bonnier de la Mosson* [175]. This belongs to the more fashionable, as opposed to the more popular, style of the time. It is, in contrast to Chardin's careful impasto, very lightly brushed. There is almost a feeling of spontaneity that is obtainable with pastel—a medium which came into prominence at just about this time. It is perhaps above all the perfect image of the enlightened private individual of elegance, culture and intellect which France produced in quantity, although the contrary impression is given by Voltaire's satire.

We come now to the period of taste and achievement in the French eighteenth century which reveals the Ancien Régime at its most attractive, and perhaps at its best. First is the *Portrait of Madame Bergeret* by François Boucher [176]. Out of a mass of heavy silks and a veritable shower of blossoms emerges the presence of a pleasant, not over-prettified, and intelligent young woman. The color of the picture is cool, the handling is swift but not in any way careless. Of almost exactly the same date, that is toward 1755, is the small marble group entitled *Venus of the Doves*

176. FRANÇOIS BOUCHER · MADAME BERGERET · WASHINGTON

by the sculptor Etienne-Maurice Falconet [177]. The figure, which recalls somewhat that of Watteau's *Ceres*, is generalized. But the head is a portrait, and without much question that of Falconet's greatest patron, the royal favorite, Madame de Pompadour. The face is not idealized, and is overcast with the effects of care and illness. The same deceptively facile presentation of surroundings as in Boucher's portrait enhances the expression of the personality of the sitter, once the seriousness of intent is recognized. The little *amours*, the forms of fish, shell and water are from the Baroque; but their treatment is mid-way between Bernini and Rodin. At this time, about the middle of the eighteenth century, there were stirring new ideas and new forms. A new chapter in feeling, as much as in political thought, was opening.

186

177. ETIENNE-MAURICE FALCONET · MADAME DE POMPADOUR AS THE VENUS OF THE DOVES
WASHINGTON

Mastery of mood and control of effect was carried by the very talented painter and illustrator, Fragonard, to larger and more ambitious aims. Two superb canvases, called *Blindman's Buff* and *The Swing* [178–181], form a pair which represent a continuous panoramic scene. They were painted toward 1775 as a kind of poetical souvenir, after Fragonard's return from a second journey to Italy, and must have been based on drawings made at the Villa d'Este at Tivoli, near Rome. It is entirely possible that the two pictures were originally one large single composition. If so, the change from the small-scale work of the earlier part of the century, such as was seen in Pater's and Lancret's canvases, is a dramatic one. Although the figure-groups in Fragonard's two paintings as they are shown today are charmingly visualized and presented, they are of

178. JEAN-HONORÉ FRAGONARD · BLINDMAN'S BUFF · WASHINGTON

secondary, or tertiary, importance. What we have here, if not the first, is very close to the grandest of all Early Romantic landscapes.

What the Romantic vision provided beyond seventeenth-century Dutch landscape [see again Pl. 149] or the fabulous reworkings of archeological data of a Ricci [see Pl. 156] was to suggest

179. Jean-Honoré Fragonard · The Swing · Washington

an active and responsive power, something like a huge soul, within the world felt, as much as seen, by man. Thus was born a fresh excitement and a vital emotional surge which sent, as in some of Fragonard's paintings like the landscape of Tivoli, a tremor at a grand scale ruffling and rippling through the forms of earth and sky, turning them into a new kind of experience

180. Detail from Plate 179

181. Detail from Plate 178

191

182. Jean-Antoine Houdon · Giuseppe Balsamo, Count Cagliostro · Washington

and design. It would seem as if the painter, some decades before Wordsworth, were impressing

> '. . . upon all forms the characters
> Of danger or desire;'

or were making

> 'The surface of the universal earth,
> With triumph and delight, with hope and fear,
> Work like a sea...'

192

183. HEAD OF COUNT CAGLIOSTRO
DETAIL FROM PLATE 182

One side of the Romantic Movement stressed a responsive Nature and with it the Natural Man. The other encouraged a new return to Rome as well as Greece. The juncture between these two poles of feeling came in the art of the sculptor Jean-Antoine Houdon, who survived the French Revolution to live well into the nineteenth century. A fine example of his ability to encompass both the aspects of natural freedom and of a Roman Revival is in the marble bust of an appropriately pre-Revolutionary Romantic subject, *Giuseppe Balsamo, Count Cagliostro* [182–183]. By the early 1780's Houdon was working in a style of strong Neo-Classical character. By 1785 the painter Jacques-Louis David had made his mark as a Neo-Classical artist of supreme stature.

David came actually later than some of his contemporaries to the subject matter of Roman history; but David's was the essential step in linking a moralistic subject of republican virtue with a stern, almost ascetic manner of painting. It was as if the uncompromising quality of realism we saw in Philippe de Champagne were being reborn along with the disinterment of the paraphernalia of Roman life uncovered from the sites of ancient Herculaneum and Pompeii. After 1800 David's style relented somewhat, but it retained, as we shall see, a quality of decision which today seems separated as if by a great gulf of feeling from the style of Boucher.

David survived the Revolution, with Houdon, to become the official court-painter of Napoleon I. The large painting entitled *Napoleon in his Study* [184] is the original of several repetitions made by the artist and was commissioned by the Marquess of Douglas. The inscription on the scroll in the shadow at the left gives the date of 1812. Here the Emperor in the green uniform of the *Chasseurs* is shown as he rises at dawn from his work table, upon which is to be seen the rolled-up *Code Napoléon* of French law. He has put aside his sword, which rests upon the ornate chair in the Antique fashion; as the candle of his lamp begins to gutter, the minute-hand of the clock moves toward a quarter past the hour of four. 'You have understood me, dear

193

184. Jacques-Louis David · Napoleon in his Study · Washington

friend', the Emperor is reported to have remarked. 'By night I work for the welfare of my subjects, and by day for their glory.' ('Vous m'avez deviné, mon cher David; la nuit je m'occupe du bonheur de mes sujets, et le jour je travaille à leur gloire.') Very possibly the trappings of symbolism, including the furniture *à la Romaine*, and anecdotal atmosphere may seem pretentious and overblown today. But there is no denying the power of the painting in projecting an image which is both persuasive and enduring.

The combination of realism and classicism was carried on well into the nineteenth century. The main figure in this particular aspect of nineteenth-century art was Jean-Dominique Ingres. Like most French artists from Poussin and Claude to his own time, he went to Rome as a young man and was entranced by what he found in the capital of the Caesars and of the Renaissance Popes. By 1813 he had forged his own style, partly from David's example but also from attentive study of the Renaissance painters, especially of his idol Raphael. The Kress Collection contains two paintings from Ingres' early Roman experience which are particularly important for our understanding of his ultimate aims. One is a superb portrait of a life-long friend, *Marcotte*—he never did a finer one [185]. Another is a scene of a papal rite in the Sistine Chapel, ordered in 1810 by Marcotte, in which behind and above the pageantry of the ceremonial are to be perceived famous Sistine frescoes by the great Renaissance forebears, including the Michelangelo of the *Last Judgment*. On returning to France Ingres enjoyed a career of public honor, for an artist almost without parallel in modern times. And from those triumphant years in France comes the final picture presented on these pages. This is from Ingres' late period, toward the middle of the nineteenth century, and represents *Madame Moitessier*, a famous beauty of her day in Paris [186, 187]. The picture is the first of two portraits of the same subject. The other, showing her in white rather than in black and seated rather than standing, is in the National Gallery in London, with an unfinished version now in Montauban (Musée Ingres).

We know something of the circumstances of the painting's creation. Ingres was struck by Madame Moitessier's sullen classic beauty. He began the portrait in 1844 but was able to finish it only in 1851. The difficulty was not so much in catching the likeness, for this one can see in scores of pencil drawings was almost like breathing to Ingres. In letters to his friend, Galibert, in 1845 and 1847 he wrote of his task as 'oppressive'. The problems of rendering in paint, not just a likeness, but a complete interpretation of a human being in a fitting environment were those which seemed to defeat him. He longed to escape to the joys of pure figure-painting, such as *L'Age d'Or*, which he was working on at this very time. 'Maudits portraits!' he wrote, '...tant un portrait est une chose difficile.' ('What a difficult thing is a portrait.') Already in Ingres' own experience the whole tenor of art was changing once again toward new aims. The individual was being lost—where is the contact with a person possible in this portrait?

It would seem almost as if Ingres had come to a point at dead center in which the capacity to find a meaningful contact with human individuality was balanced by the dominance of type and generality. This is fundamentally the great problem raised by Classic art, beginning with Greek times, in the Western world. It is not enough merely to talk about the importance of the individual. It is necessary also to find him, to locate him as a personal force within the general principles of humanity which dignify and, in a way, justify his existence. Possibly Raphael at one time had met the same dilemma. Perhaps on such a fundamental point began the drama of development in Western Art which we have followed through these selected examples in the Kress Collection from the early fourteenth century to the year 1851.

At the beginning of this essay I suggested a close parallel between the ideal of a nineteenth-century American as a collector of art for the American people and the program of the Kress

185. JEAN-AUGUSTE-DOMINIQUE INGRES · M. MARCOTTE · WASHINGTON

Collection and Foundation. But to the reader who has come this far it must be abundantly evident that the Kress Collection is of such vastly greater magnitude in all respects that further comparison soon loses all point. It would be, in a way, to compare the acorn with the oak.

186. Jean-Auguste-Dominique Ingres · Madame Moitessier · Washington

187. HEAD OF MADAME MOITESSIER · DETAIL FROM PLATE 186

The true conclusion of this essay should not be concerned with the past but with the future. In its planning and making the Kress Collection has been in the good tradition of a 'citizens' collection'. Its usefulness and value can be no less than the interests and insights it may inspire among American citizens over the breadth of the country at large. Among its contributions may be the gift of new and vivid ways of grasping the heritage they are fortunate in possessing in the Western tradition and of seeing more plainly the vitality of works of art in that tradition—by artists whom they may come to know, not as names in an encyclopedia, but as 'men who have traveled before them the same long road in which they walk'.[30]

NOTES

NOTES

1. Captain Frederick Marryat, novelist, naval officer and author of *A Diary in America*, Philadelphia, 1839. See Allan Nevins, *American Social History as recorded by British Travellers*, New York, 1923, p. 245.

2. See Theodore Sizer, article on Jarves in the *American Dictionary of Biography;* also Francis Steegmuller, *The Two Lives of James Jackson Jarves*, New Haven, Yale University Press, 1952.

3. The painting shows a manuscript codex of Dante's *Paradiso* open to a page of Canto XXV, where may be read a famous passage beginning with the words 'Se mai continga...' (If it should ever happen...) and continues to express the hope that the poet would be one day welcomed back from exile to his native Florence; in fact, to be made poet laureate in the very Baptistry opposite the Cathedral where he was baptized as an infant. The Kress Collection ideal portrait has only fairly recently been rediscovered in an English collection, and the attribution to Pontormo may possibly be altered by specialists to another Florentine painter of the same period, such as Bacchiacca (see Pl. 103).

4. For Cennino Cennini, see D. V. Thompson's translated edition, *The Craftsman's Handbook*, recently reissued in paperback by Dover Publications. For Giotto's fame, see the quotations given in Peter Murray, *Sources for Italian Art before Vasari*, Florence, 1959. Often later writers attributed to Giotto some of the qualities of their own times and tastes; a good example is Ghiberti.

5. The style of the Kress Collection *Annunciation* figures is very close to that of the *Madonna*, in marble, in the Church of the Annunziata at Trapani in Sicily. The Trapani *Madonna*, imported at an uncertain date from Pisa, was specified as the model for a marble *Madonna and Child* by Laurana as late as 1461 (see S. Bottari in *La Critica d'Arte*, 1956, pp. 555–557) and again in 1503. Not all scholars attribute the S. Caterina, Pisa, figures to Nino Pisano (for one, Professor Martin Weinberger in *The Art Bulletin*, 1937, pp. 86 ff.). It is possible that the related Kress figures represent a Pisan or Lucchese link between Nino and the slightly later art of the young Quercia.

6. For an example of Quercia's carving before 1400 see a Madonna now on the Piccolomini altar in the Siena Duomo proposed by Enzo Carli in *Critica d'Arte*, 1949, pp. 17 ff. The case for Quercia's authorship of the Kress *Madonna of Humility* is given by Hanns Swarzenski and myself in *Gazette des Beaux-Arts*, 1946, pp. 129–152. An alternative attribution is given by John Pope-Hennessy, *Italian Gothic Sculpture*, London-New York, 1955, with a bibliographical summary.

7. The anonymous Master of the Osservanza (to whom the painting from the St. Anthony Altar illustrated in Pl. 17 is attributed by several scholars) is so called because the work which seems to give most precisely his artistic personality is a large altarpiece in the Church of the Osservanza, situated just outside the city walls of Siena. The problem of the authorship of the St. Anthony Altar is still unresolved although it must fairly be said that among interested scholars adherents to the idea that it should be attributed (at least in large part) to the 'Master of the Osservanza Altarpiece' rather than to Sassetta seem to be growing rather than diminishing at this writing.

8. See L. B. Alberti, *Della Pittura* (Italian version of 1436, dedicated to Brunelleschi): ed. Malle, Florence 1951; ed. and transl. J. R. Spencer, Oxford-New Haven, 1956.

9. For the importance of the visual sequences of form in the reconstruction of the St. Lucy Altar predella I am indebted to Professor Helmut Wohl, who is preparing a full-scale monograph on Domenico.

10. The attribution to Ghiberti was originally made by von Bode over fifty years ago. It is accepted by John Pope-Hennessy (*Italian Gothic Sculpture*, 1955). The whole group of undocumented terracottas, of which this is probably the outstanding example, was not included in the modern authoritative study of the sculptor by Professor Richard Krautheimer (*Lorenzo Ghiberti*, Princeton, 1956).

11. The identification of the bust as of Simonetta Vespucci and the attribution to Leonardo are due to the late Dr. W. E. Suida (*Art Quarterly*, 1947).

12. There may not be not complete agreement of opinion on the date of this particular portrait-bust, that is, whether it belongs to Verrocchio's lifetime or to that of the next generation. Some see the evidence of Verrocchio's own hand in analogy, perhaps, to the head of the Colleone Monument and on the basis of style and quality the bust is clearly the finest of several known variants.

13. There has been difficulty in attributing the piece on a purely stylistic basis either to Pisanello or to his most gifted follower in the medallic art, Matteo de' Pasti; a recent study reaffirms the current attribution to Alberti himself (originally Hill's): Kurt Badt, in *Mitteilungen des Kunsthistorischen Instituts in Florenz*, 1958, pp. 78–87.

14. The style is not that of Pietro Lombardo, as I must confess I once thought, and in error wrote; it is really much more subtle and more closely fits the style of his greatly gifted and more poetic son, Antonio. See *Masterpieces of Sculpture in the National Gallery of Art*; there the description mentions the fact that the arms of the figure were broken after the marble was calcined by fire. It seems possible that this piece is a survivor of two candelabrum-bearing angels from the altar of the beautiful church of Santa Maria dei Miracoli, in Venice, which were believed to have been destroyed by a fire which attacked the choir of the church. The sculpture of the church was executed mainly by the young Antonio and Tullio Lombardo under the direction of their father, Pietro.

15. Max J. Friedländer, *Die Altniederländische Malerei*, VI, p. 55 ff. quoted and translated by Erwin Panofsky, *Early Netherlandish Painting*, Cambridge, Harvard University Press, 1953, p. 348.

16. Two other panels from the original altarpiece probably destined for the Royal Abbey at St. Denis are now in the National Gallery in London. These panels still present on their reverses paintings of St. Peter and St. Rémy in neutral tints *(grisaille)*. The Kress Collection panels no longer have any paintings on their reverses, but it is presumed that they must have had originally figures of St. Denis and St. Gilles. No other painter and no other painting have quite the same close connection with Paris and the French Monarchy toward 1500.

17. A detailed analysis of the instruments in this picture has been made by Dr. Emmanuel Winternitz, of the Metropolitan Museum of Art, New York. It is quoted in part here: 'The arrangement is carefully divided into two orchestras, one surrounding Mary and represented in larger size; the other smaller, surrounding the throne of the Holy Trinity.

   'The musicians surrounding Mary consist of a quartet of singers and of seven instrumentalists with an interesting combination of winds and strings. The angel at the upper left plays an alto shawm... The next angel to the right plays a standard harp, of typically Gothic design, with twenty strings. Of the corresponding two angels at the right, the left one is playing a discant shawm, the other a typical vielle of the time... The angel on the middle left holds a trumpet (only upper part visible), the angel beneath plays a portative organ with thirty-six metal pipes arranged in two rows... The corresponding pair of angels at the right play a discant shawm and a small lute...

   'The inner circle of musicians about the throne is just as carefully organized, with a choir of eleven singers at the left and a small orchestra of six instrumentalists equally divided into winds and strings at the right... All the instruments are contemporary with the painting and depicted with the greatest exactness as if the artist had transplanted into Heaven a musical performance of his own time. Equally precise is the rendering of the finger positions, the holding of the bow, etc. Also, the organization of the two orchestras and their quantitative relation to small vocal groups is by no means fanciful; it is quite in line with contemporary practice.'

18. The dating before 1500 after Dürer's first Italian trip is that proposed by the Kress Foundation, the National Gallery of Art and the great majority of authorities on Dürer, including Erwin Panofsky (see his *Albrecht Dürer*, II, Princeton, 1943, p. 10, with citation of differing opinion by E. Buchner, 1943). The deciphering of the coats of arms on the obverse is needed badly however as further element of proof. The relationship of the figure-style on the reverse to Dürer's studio would appear also to need more investigation, which in turn could lead to a reconsideration of the date. In any event the painting is one of the key-elements in any view of the effect of Dürer's Italian experiences on his art.

19. This ranks with the very finest individual bronze reliefs of the Renaissance in this country. It is not documented; and its date, its original setting and its planned function are alike unknown. The attribution, based largely on the pose, proportions and some elements of surface effects, is usually to the Sienese sculptor Francesco di Giorgio. The proliferation of detail and the discrepancy in scale between lion, hat and figure, on the other hand, are quite alien to Francesco di Giorgio's way of thinking. It is possible that we have here the work of a North Italian who had come into contact with Tuscan influences, such as the well known sculptor in bronze, Bartolommeo Bellano of Padua. If this should prove correct, the Kress plaque would be virtually his masterpiece.

20. The portrait was given most recently in the catalogue of the recent Holbein Exhibition in Basel to Ambrosius Holbein, Hans the Younger's elder brother, who died probably in 1519 (see P. H. Boerlin, in *Die Malerfamilie Holbein in Basel*, Basel Kunstmuseum, 1960, p. 134). This is a revival of an attribution disputed in 1931 by Baldass. According to this opinion the mood of the portrait is too 'subjective' and the color not 'usual' for Hans the Younger. This is still not conclusive stylistic evidence against the attribution to the early years of Hans the Younger, when the influence of his brother might be more to be expected than not.

21. The problem of authorship presented by the two pictures attributed to Giorgione in the Kress Collection is still not fully resolved. However, the group to which some feel they both belong, called the 'Allendale Group' (after the *Adoration of the Shepherds* or *Nativity* which was in the Allendale Collection before it came to the Kress Collection) is receiving more support as time goes on as from Giorgione's own hand. In a cable to the Kress Foundation just before his death in 1959, Bernard Berenson stated his final belief that the Allendale-Kress *Ado-*

ration of the Shepherds was entirely by Giorgione. Earlier he had published his opinion that the painting was by Titian or finished by Titian on Giorgione's design. See also Cecil Gould, *National Gallery Catalogues* (London), *The Sixteenth-Century Venetian School*, 1959, pp. 35–39.

22. A portrait of the poet Jacopo Sannazaro by Giovanni Paolo de Agostini is in the Kress Collection of the Isaac Delgado Museum, New Orleans.

23. Vasari's text is not free of ambiguities so that critics and scholars today are forced back to the data of style in the painting itself. In opposition to the theory of Raphael's authorship there is current the alternative that the picture was painted by the chief disciple in Raphael's Roman shop, Giulio Romano. A persuasive recent exposition of this view is given by Professor Frederick Hartt, *Giulio Romano*, New Haven, 1959, pp. 51–53.

24. Recently there has come a suggestion for the identity of the man portrayed in this picture: Francesco dell'Ajolle, a famous Florentine musician, whose portrait was at one time in the Riccardi family-collection (H. Keutner, in *Mitteilungen des Kunsthistorischen Instituts in Florenz*, 1959, pp. 142, 143). This theory supposes that the empty left hand was originally intended to hold a lyre, symbol of the subject's calling in life. It is quite possible that the painting was never carried to completion, being left as finished in the main essentials only, on the departure of Rosso for France to become *peintre du roi* at the French Court.

25. The sources tell us that Caravaggio was noted for his painting of fruit and vegetables and for a time made his way on sales of these subjects. Whether these were straight still-life or studies of figure with still-life is not certain. The attribution of the Kress picture to Caravaggio was first made by Professor Roberto Longhi in 1928, and has since received support, though not unanimously, by specialists, for example, not by Professor Walter Friedländer (*Caravaggio Studies*, Princeton, 1955).

26. The foreshortened head of the saint is more reminiscent of several heads by Giulio Romano in his frescoes in the Palazzo del Te decorated for the Gonzaga than those of Titian's ceiling paintings now in the Salute, Venice. Titian was also employed by the Gonzaga in 1534–1537 in the decoration of the Ducal Palace within the city of Mantua. It may be that the Kress painting represents a chromatic and tonal solution to the problem of ceiling decoration which Titian might have observed Giulio Romano at grips with, though the dating of the Kress canvas is given usually as 1530–1535—that is, somewhat before Titian's paintings for the Palace in Mantua. A link between the art of Titian and that of Giulio Romano may be supposed because of the enthusiasm of Pietro Aretino (Titian's great admirer) for Giulio's talents.

27. Vouet's painting of the Muses was first published with a treatment of its relations to a whole group with similar subject matter and style, by Robert L. Manning in *Studies in the History of Art, Dedicated to W. E. Suida on his Eightieth Birthday*, published by the Phaidon Press for the Samuel H. Kress Foundation, 1959, pp. 297–300. I am grateful to Professor William Crelly, who has prepared a monograph on Vouet, for his views on Vouet's shift to his 'French' manner after his return to France from Italy.

28. The identification of the eldest of the standing figures to the left (in Polish costume) as Franciscus Salesius Count Potocki was made recently by Professor Stanislas Lorentz, Director of the Warsaw Museum, who communicated his findings to the late Dr. W. E. Suida of the Kress Foundation. The 'palace' seems certainly to be an ideal structure, not a building that was ever actually constructed. Variations on this 'palace' theme, some connected with the Polish royal family, are known: see H. A. Fritsche, *Bernardo Bellotto genannt Canaletto*, Marburg, 1936; T. Borenius, in *Burlington Magazine*, 1921, and *Dedalo*, 1922.

29. The passage quoted is from Diderot's *Essay on Painting*, translated by Creighton Gilbert, in E. G. Holt, *A Documentary History of Art*, Doubleday-Anchor, 1958, II, p. 314.

30. James Jackson Jarves, *Art Hints*, New York, 1855, p. 326.

CIMA DA CONEGLIANO
Venetian, c. 1459–1517/18

ST. HELENA. Panel, $15\frac{3}{4} \times 12\frac{5}{8}$ in. (40,2 × 32,2 cm.).
Painted soon after 1500.   *Plates 50–51*

Provenance: Ellen Sydney, daughter of the Viscount of Strangford; George John, Marquess of Sligo, Westport House, County Mayo, Ireland; Lady Isabel Mary Peyronet Browne, London; Dr. James Hasson, London; Samuel H. Kress Collection, 1954 (K 2001).
WASHINGTON, D.C., National Gallery of Art (1369).

FRANÇOIS CLOUET
French, c. 1510–1572

«DIANE DE POITIERS». Panel, $36\frac{1}{4} \times 32$ in. (92,1 × 81,3 cm.).
                                        Plates 105–107
Inscribed, below the left hand of the lady: FR. IANETII OPVS.
Painted c. 1550.

Provenance: Sir Richard Frederick, Burwood Park; Cook Collection, Richmond, Surrey; Samuel H. Kress Collection, 1955 (K 2125).
WASHINGTON, D.C., National Gallery of Art (1370).

FRANCESCO DEL COSSA
Ferrarese, c. 1435–1477

ST. LUCY. Panel, $31\frac{1}{4} \times 22$ in. (79 × 56 cm.).   *Plate 42*
Painted 1470/77.

Provenance: Spiridon Collection, Paris; Samuel H. Kress Collection, 1936 (K 417).
WASHINGTON, D.C., National Gallery of Art (339).

THE CRUCIFIXION. Panel; tondo, diam. 25 in. (63,5 cm.).
                                        Plate 45

Provenance: Constabili Collection, Ferrara, Italy; Philip Lehman, New York; Samuel H. Kress Collection, 1943 (K 1361).
WASHINGTON, D.C., National Gallery of Art (793).

ANTOINE COYSEVOX
French, 1640–1720

LOUIS OF FRANCE, THE GRAND DAUPHIN. Marble, without base: $31 \times 29\frac{1}{2} \times 13\frac{3}{8}$ in. (78,7 × 74,9 × 34 cm.).   *Plate 169*

Provenance: Château de Condé; Sir Richard Wallace, Château de Bagatelle, Paris; Lord Hertford; John Murray Scott; Lady Sackville West; Princesse de Faucigny-Lucinge; Samuel H. Kress Collection, 1951 (K 1841).
WASHINGTON, D.C., National Gallery of Art (A–1649).

LUCAS CRANACH, THE ELDER
German, 1472–1553

MADONNA AND CHILD. Panel, $48 \times 35\frac{3}{4}$ in. (121,9 × 90,9 cm.).   *Plate 78*
Painted in 1513.

Provenance: Max Freiherr von Hely, Darmstadt; Frau A. Ullmann, Frankfurt am Main; Samuel H. Kress Collection, 1948 (K 1595).
TUCSON, Arizona, University of Arizona.

DONATO CRETI
School of Bologna, 1671–1747

THE QUARREL. Canvas, 51×40 in. (129,5 × 101,6 cm.).
Painted before 1739.   *Plate 158*

Provenance: Conte Pietro Ercole Fava, Bologna, Italy; Samuel H. Kress Collection, 1952 (K 1880).
WASHINGTON, D.C., National Gallery of Art (1363).

CARLO CRIVELLI
Venetian, 1430/35–c. 1493

MADONNA AND CHILD ENTHRONED WITH DONOR. Panel, $51 \times 21\frac{3}{8}$ in. (129,5 × 54,5 cm.).   *Plate 48*

Provenance: The Earl of Dudley; Sir Herbert Cook, Richmond, Surrey; Sir Francis Cook, Richmond, Surrey; Samuel H. Kress Collection, 1944 (K 1383).
WASHINGTON, D.C., National Gallery of Art (794).

JACQUES-LOUIS DAVID
French, 1748–1825

NAPOLEON IN HIS STUDY. Canvas, $80\frac{1}{4} \times 49\frac{1}{4}$ in. (203,9 × 125,1 cm.).   *Plate 184*
Signed and dated, on a scroll at lower left: «LVD.^{ci} DAVID OPVS 1812.»

Provenance: Marquess of Douglas, Duke of Hamilton, Hamilton Palace, near Glasgow (Scotland); Earl of Rosebery, London; Samuel H. Kress Collection, 1954 (K 2046).
WASHINGTON, D.C., National Gallery of Art (1374).

DESIDERIO DA SETTIGNANO
Florentine, 1428–1464

THE CHRIST CHILD. Marble, $12 \times 10\frac{7}{16} \times 6\frac{7}{16}$ in. (30,5 × 26,5 × 16,3 cm.).   *Plate 32*
Datable toward 1460.

Provenance: From the Church of San Francesco dei Vanchetoni, Florence, Italy; Samuel H. Kress Collection, 1942 (K 1309).
WASHINGTON, D.C., National Gallery of Art (A–148).

BUST OF A LADY. Marble, $20\frac{7}{8} \times 19\frac{3}{16} \times 7\frac{13}{16}$ in. (53 × 48,8 × 19,9 cm.).   *Plate 37*
About 1460.

Provenance: Alessandro Castellani, Rome, Italy; Arthur de Schickler, Martivaast, France; Count Hubert de Pourtalès, Paris; Clarence H. Mackay, Roslyn, L.I., New York; Samuel H. Kress Collection, 1936 (K SF5F).
WASHINGTON, D.C., National Gallery of Art (A–30).

DOMENICO VENEZIANO
Florentine, c. 1400–1461

ST. JOHN IN THE DESERT. Panel, $11\frac{1}{8} \times 12\frac{3}{4}$ in. ($28,5 \times 32,5$ cm.). *Plate* 28

Provenance: Bernard Berenson, Florence, Italy; Carl W. Hamilton, New York; Samuel H. Kress Collection, 1942 (K 1331).
WASHINGTON, D.C., National Gallery of Art (715).

ST. FRANCIS RECEIVING THE STIGMATA. Panel, $10\frac{1}{4} \times 11\frac{7}{8}$ in. (26×30 cm.). *Plate* 29
Painted c. 1450.

Provenance: From the Altarpiece of Santa Lucia de' Magnoli, Florence; Contini Bonacossi Collection, Florence; Samuel H. Kress Collection, 1933 (K 278).
WASHINGTON, D.C., National Gallery of Art (251).

MADONNA AND CHILD. Panel, $32\frac{1}{2} \times 22\frac{1}{4}$ in. (83×57 cm.).
Painted c. 1450. *Plate* 30

Provenance: Professor Edgeworth, Edgeworthstown, Ireland; Samuel H. Kress Collection, 1936 (K 410).
WASHINGTON, D.C., National Gallery of Art (332).

DUCCIO DI BUONINSEGNA
Sienese, active 1278–1319

THE CALLING OF THE APOSTLES PETER AND ANDREW. Panel, $17\frac{1}{16} \times 18\frac{3}{16}$ in. ($43,5 \times 46$ cm.). *Plate* 4
Painted 1308/11.

Provenance: Benson Collection, London; Clarence H. Mackay, Roslyn, L.I., New York; Samuel H. Kress Collection, 1934 (K 283).
WASHINGTON, D.C., National Gallery of Art (252).

ALBRECHT DÜRER
German, 1471–1528

PORTRAIT OF A CLERGYMAN. Parchment on canvas, $16\frac{15}{16} \times 13$ in. (43×33 cm.). *Plate* 72
Signed with Dürer's monogram and dated 1516, on parchment.

Provenance: Paul de Praun, Nürnberg, Germany; Count Johann Rudolf Czernin von Chudenitz, Vienna, Austria; Samuel H. Kress Collection, 1950 (K 1702).
WASHINGTON, D.C., National Gallery of Art (1100).

MADONNA AND CHILD (Obv.); LOT AND HIS DAUGHTERS (Rev.). Panel, $19\frac{3}{4} \times 15\frac{5}{8}$ in. ($50,2 \times 39,7$ cm.).
Dürer's monogram in the Lot scene. *Plates* 73–74
Painted c. 1497/98.

Provenance: Colonel a'Court Repington, London; Mrs. Phyllis Loder; Baron Heinrich Thyssen-Bornemisza, Schloss Rohoncz, Lugano, Switzerland; Samuel H. Kress Collection, 1950 (K 1835).
WASHINGTON, D.C., National Gallery of Art (1099).

ANTHONY VAN DYCK
Flemish, 1599–1641

QUEEN HENRIETTA MARIA WITH HER DWARF. Canvas, $86\frac{1}{4} \times 53\frac{1}{8}$ in. ($219,1 \times 134,8$ cm.). *Plates* 139–140
Painted c. 1633.

Provenance: The Earls of Bradford; Diana, Countess of Mountrath; Milton Abbey, Earl of Dorchester; Earl of Portarlington, Emo Park, Queen's County, Ireland (1878); Earls of Northbrook (1881–1927); William Randolph Hearst, Los Angeles, California; Samuel H. Kress Collection, 1952 (K 1911).
WASHINGTON, D.C., National Gallery of Art (1118).

ÉTIENNE-MAURICE FALCONET
French, 1716–1791

MADAME POMPADOUR AS THE VENUS OF THE DOVES. Marble, $29\frac{1}{2} \times 28 \times 18$ in. ($75 \times 71,1 \times 45,7$ cm.). *Plate* 177
After 1755/57.

Provenance: Comte de Parabère; Comte de Lamoignon; Comte Trudaine de Montigny; Duc de Cambacerès, Paris; Samuel H. Kress Collection, 1946 (K 1423).
WASHINGTON, D.C., National Gallery of Art (A–1625).

JEAN-HONORÉ FRAGONARD
French, 1732–1806

BLINDMAN'S BUFF. Canvas, $85\frac{1}{8} \times 77\frac{7}{8}$ in. ($216,2 \times 197,8$ cm.). *Plates* 178, 181
THE SWING. Canvas, 85×73 in. ($215,9 \times 185,5$ cm.). *Plates* 179, 180
Painted c. 1765.

Provenance: Marquis de Cypierre; Camille Groult, Paris; Samuel H. Kress Collection, 1954 (K 2050, K 2051).
WASHINGTON, D.C., National Gallery of Art (1377, 1376).

FRANCESCO DI GIORGIO
Sienese, 1439–1502

ST. JEROME. Bronze, $21\frac{5}{8} \times 14\frac{11}{16} \times 1\frac{7}{16}$ in. ($55 \times 37,5 \times 3,7$ cm.). *Plate* 81

Provenance: Eugène Piot, Paris; Gustave Dreyfus, Paris; Samuel H. Kress Collection, 1944 (K 1379.2C).
WASHINGTON, D.C., National Gallery of Art (A–165.2C).

GENTILE DA FABRIANO
Umbrian, c. 1360–1427

MADONNA AND CHILD. Panel, $37\frac{3}{4} \times 22\frac{1}{4}$ in. (96×57 cm.).
Painted c. 1420. *Plate* 7

Provenance: Madame E. J. Sartoris, Paris; Goldman Collection, New York; Samuel H. Kress Collection, 1937 (K 472).
WASHINGTON, D.C., National Gallery of Art (366).

LIST OF PLATES

LIST OF PLATES

LEON BATTISTA ALBERTI
Florentine, 1404–1472

SELF-PORTRAIT. Bronze, black patina, $7\frac{29}{32} \times 5\frac{11}{32} \times \frac{5}{8}$ in. (20,1 × 13,6 × 0,15 cm.). *Plate 40*
Inscribed: L. BAP. (the stops shaped like eyes).

Provenance: Vicomte de Janzé, Paris; Charles Timbal, Paris; Gustave Dreyfus, Paris; Samuel H. Kress Collection, 1944 (K 1379.1B).
WASHINGTON, D.C., National Gallery of Art (A–278.1B).

FRA ANGELICO
Florentine, 1387–1455

THE HEALING OF PALLADIA BY ST. COSMAS AND ST. DAMIAN. Panel, $14\frac{3}{8} \times 18\frac{5}{8}$ in. (36,5 × 47,5 cm.).
About 1439/40. *Plates 22, 24*

Provenance: Sir John Rushout, Bart., first Lord Northwich, Thirlestane House, Cheltenham, Gloucestershire, England; Samuel H. Kress Collection, 1944 (K 1387).
WASHINGTON, D.C., National Gallery of Art (790).

FRA ANGELICO and FRA FILIPPO LIPPI
Florentine School, 1387–1455; c. 1406–1469

THE ADORATION OF THE MAGI. Tondo, panel (poplar), Diameter 54 in. (137,2 cm.). *Plates 19–21*

Provenance: From the estate of Lorenzo de' Medici to the Guicciardini Palace, Florence; William Coningham, London; W. Brown (1848); Alexander Barker (1854); Cook Collection, Richmond, Surrey (1874); Samuel H. Kress Collection, 1947 (K 1425).
WASHINGTON, D.C., National Gallery of Art (1085).

BACCHIACCA
Florentine, 1494–1557

THE GATHERING OF THE MANNA. Panel, $44 \times 37\frac{1}{2}$ in. (112 × 95 cm.). *Plates 103–104*
Painted about 1545/55.

Provenance: Stefano Bardini, Florence, Italy; Samuel H. Kress Collection, 1943 (K 1362).
WASHINGTON, D.C., National Gallery of Art (791).

GIOVANNI BELLINI
Venetian, c. 1430–1516

ST. JEROME READING. Panel, $19\frac{1}{4} \times 15\frac{1}{2}$ in. (49 × 39 cm.).
Plates 52–53

Provenance: Lord Monson, Reigate, Surrey, England; Robert and Evelyn Benson, London; Clarence H. Mackay, Roslyn,

L. I., New York; Samuel H. Kress Collection, 1936 (K 406).
WASHINGTON, D.C., National Gallery of Art (328).

MADONNA AND CHILD. Transferred from panel to canvas, $29\frac{1}{8} \times 22\frac{1}{4}$ in. (74 × 56,5 cm.). *Plate 54*
Signed on the parapet: IOANNES BELLINVS.
Painted c. 1485/90.

Provenance: Conde de Montijo, Madrid (until 1870); Otto Mündler, Paris; Grand Duke of Oldenburg, Germany; Mrs. Nicholas F. Brady, Manhasset, L . I., New York; Samuel H. Kress Collection, 1952 (K 1905).
KANSAS CITY, Missouri, The William Rockhill Nelson Gallery and Mary Atkins Museum of Fine Arts.

BERNARDO BELLOTTO
Venetian, 1720–1780

ENTRANCE TO A PALACE. Canvas, $61\frac{3}{8} \times 45\frac{3}{8}$ in. (155,9 × 115,2 cm.). *Plate 165*
Signed in the lower right corner: «Bernard. BELOTTO DE CANALETTO.»

Provenance: Colonel Robert Adeane, O. B. E., Babraham Hall, Cambridge, England; Samuel H. Kress Collection, 1950 (K 1691).
EL PASO, Texas, El Paso Museum of Art.

BENEDETTO DA MAIANO
Florentine, 1442–1497

MADONNA AND CHILD. Marble, $22\frac{7}{8} \times 15\frac{1}{4} \times 3\frac{7}{8}$ in. (58,2 × 38,7 × 9,8 cm.). *Plate 31*
About 1485.

Provenance: The Princes Liechtenstein, since Johannes II (reigned 1858–1929); Samuel H. Kress Collection, 1953 (K 1976).
WASHINGTON, D.C., National Gallery of Art (A–1661).

GIAN LORENZO BERNINI
Roman, 1598–1680

MONSIGNOR FRANCESCO BARBERINI. Marble, $31\frac{1}{8} \times 26 \times 10\frac{1}{2}$ in. (79,2 × 66,1 × 26,7 cm.). *Plates 143–144*

Provenance: The Barberini Family, Rome, Italy; Samuel H. Kress Collection, 1951 (K 1828).
WASHINGTON, D.C., National Gallery of Art (A–1646).

PARIS BORDONE
Venetian, 1500–1571

YOUNG HERO ARMED BY BELLONA AND MERCURY. Canvas, $41 \times 60\frac{3}{4}$ in. (104 × 154,5 cm.). *Plates 111–112*
Signed: Paridis / Bord.
Painted c. 1535/45.

Provenance: Edward Solly, Esq., London; Cook Collection, Richmond, Surrey; Samuel H. Kress Collection, 1949 (K 1631).
BIRMINGHAM, Alabama, Birmingham Museum of Art.

HIERONYMUS BOSCH
Flemish, c. 1450–1516

DEATH AND THE MISER. Panel, $36\frac{5}{8} \times 12\frac{1}{8}$ in. (93×31 cm.).
Plates 70–71

Provenance: Private Collection, Ireland; Baron Joseph van der Elst, Château d'Ostkerke (near Bruges), Belgium; Samuel H. Kress Collection, 1951 (K 1848).
WASHINGTON, D.C., National Gallery of Art (1112).

SANDRO BOTTICELLI
Florentine, 1444–1510

GIULIANO DE' MEDICI. Panel, $29\frac{3}{4} \times 20\frac{5}{8}$ in. ($75,6 \times 52,6$ cm.).
Plate 38

Provenance: Private Collection, Italy; Samuel H. Kress Collection, 1949 (K 1644).
WASHINGTON, D.C., National Gallery of Art (1135).

FRANÇOIS BOUCHER
French, 1703–1770

MADAME BERGERET. Canvas, $56\frac{1}{4} \times 41\frac{3}{8}$ in. (143×105 cm.). Signed and dated: «F. Boucher 1746».
Plate 176

Provenance: Jacques Onésime Bergeret (until 1785), Paris; Pierre Jacques Bergeret (until 1827); Ange Philippe de la Girennerie; Poisson de la Chabeaussière; Cotillon de Torcy; Contre-Admiral Le Bos de Sainte Croix; Comte Fontaine de Resbecq; Samuel H. Kress Collection, 1945 (K 1335).
WASHINGTON, D.C., National Gallery of Art (768).

PIETER BRUEGEL, THE ELDER
Flemish, c. 1525–1569

THE TEMPTATION OF ST. ANTHONY. Panel, $23 \times 33\frac{3}{4}$ in. ($58,4 \times 85,7$ cm.).
Plates 84–85
Painted about 1557/58.

Provenance: Countess Montblanc, Belgium; Samuel H. Kress Collection, 1950 (K 1701).
WASHINGTON, D.C., National Gallery of Art (1102).

CANALETTO
Venetian, 1697–1768

THE PORTELLO AND THE BRENTA CANAL AT PADUA. Canvas, $24\frac{1}{4} \times 42\frac{5}{8}$ in. ($61,6 \times 108,3$ cm.).
Plates 161–162

Provenance: F. Madan, Esq., England; Samuel H. Kress Collection, 1957 (K 2175).
WASHINGTON, D.C., National Gallery of Art (1605).

MICHELANGELO DA CARAVAGGIO
Roman, 1573–1610

STILL LIFE. Canvas, $19\frac{7}{8} \times 28$ in. (51×72 cm.). *Plate 108*

Provenance: Fejer de Buck, Rome, Italy; Samuel H. Kress Collection, 1935 (K 306).
WASHINGTON, D.C., National Gallery of Art (270).

ANNIBALE CARRACCI
School of Bologna, 1560–1609

VENUS ADORNED BY THE GRACES. Canvas, transferred from wood, $52\frac{3}{8} \times 67\frac{1}{8}$ in. ($133 \times 170,5$ cm.).
Plate 129
Before 1595.

Provenance: Casa Tanari (1678), Bologna, Italy; Hugh A. J. Munro, Novar, Scotland; Mr. Dyer (1878); Cook Collection, Richmond, Surrey; Samuel H. Kress Collection, 1949 (K 1622).
WASHINGTON, D.C., National Gallery of Art (1366).

GIACOMO CERUTI
Brescian, active in the second quarter of the 18th Century

THE CARD GAME. Canvas, $28\frac{1}{2} \times 40\frac{3}{4}$ in. ($72,4 \times 103,5$ cm.).
Plate 153

Samuel H. Kress Collection, 1957 (K 2182).
RALEIGH, North Carolina, North Carolina Museum of Art.

PHILIPPE DE CHAMPAGNE
French, 1602–1674

OMER TALON. Canvas, $88\frac{1}{2} \times 63\frac{5}{8}$ in. ($225 \times 161,6$ cm.).
Plates 141–142
Signed and dated: «Ph. de Champagne fecit Anno 1649 aetatis 54. »

Provenance: Avocat Général Omer Talon, Paris; Joly de Fleury; De Buttet Family, Bourget du Lac, Savoye, France; Samuel H. Kress Collection, 1950 (K 1837).
WASHINGTON, D.C., National Gallery of Art (1114).

JEAN-BAPTISTE-SIMÉON CHARDIN
French, 1699–1779

THE KITCHEN MAID. Canvas, $18\frac{1}{8} \times 14\frac{3}{4}$ in. ($46,2 \times 37,5$ cm.).
Plate 174

Provenance: The Princes Liechtenstein (from 1747), Vaduz, Liechtenstein; Samuel H. Kress Collection, 1951 (K 1847).
WASHINGTON, D.C., National Gallery of Art (1117).

Companion piece, also in the Kress Collection (K 1838): *The Attentive Nurse*, Washington, D.C., National Gallery of Art (1116).

PETRUS CHRISTUS
Flemish, c. 1410–1472/73

A DONOR; WIFE OF THE DONOR. Two panels, each $16\frac{1}{2} \times 8\frac{1}{2}$ in. ($42 \times 21,6$ cm.).
Plates 63–64
Painted c. 1460.

Provenance: Formerly in a Genoese family; Samuel H. Kress Collection, 1937 (K 488A, 488B).
WASHINGTON, D.C., National Gallery of Art (1367, 1368).

ORAZIO GENTILESCHI
Tuscan (Pisa), 1543–1627

PORTRAIT OF A YOUNG WOMAN. Canvas, $31\frac{3}{8} \times 28\frac{1}{4}$ in. (79,8 × 71,8 cm.). *Plate* 131

Provenance: Private Collection, England; Samuel H. Kress Collection, 1953 (K 1949).
HOUSTON, Texas, Museum of Fine Arts.

LORENZO GHIBERTI
Florentine, 1378–1455

MADONNA AND CHILD. Terracotta, painted, $40\frac{3}{8} \times 24\frac{1}{2} \times 11\frac{1}{8}$ in. (102,5 × 62,2 × 28,3 cm.). *Plate* 36

Provenance: Dr. Eduard Simon, Berlin, Germany; Clarence H. Mackay, Roslyn, L.I., N.Y.; Samuel H. Kress Collection, 1941 (K 1278).
WASHINGTON, D.C., National Gallery of Art (A–147).

DOMENICO GHIRLANDAIO
Florentine, 1449–1494

MADONNA AND CHILD. Panel (transferred to masonite), $28\frac{7}{8} \times 20$ in. (73,4 × 50,8 cm.). *Plate* 35
Painted c. 1470/75.

Provenance: Mrs. E. L. Scott, London; Samuel H. Kress Collection, 1954 (K 2076).
WASHINGTON, D.C., National Gallery of Art (1412).

GIORGIONE
Venetian, c. 1478–1510

THE ADORATION OF THE SHEPHERDS. Panel, $35\frac{3}{4} \times 43\frac{1}{2}$ in. (91 × 111 cm.). *Plates* 86, 88, 89
Painted 1500/5.

Provenance: Cardinal Fesch Collection, Rome; Claudius Tarral (1841); T. Wentworth Beaumont (1847); Lord Allendale, London; Samuel H. Kress Collection, 1938 (K 509).
WASHINGTON, D.C., National Gallery of Art (400).

THE HOLY FAMILY. Panel, $14\frac{5}{8} \times 17\frac{7}{8}$ in. (37,3 × 45,6 cm.). *Plate* 87

Provenance: Henry Willet, Brighton, England; Robert R. and Evelyn Benson, London; Samuel H. Kress Collection, 1949 (K 1660).
WASHINGTON, D.C., National Gallery of Art (1091).

GIOTTO
Florentine, c. 1266–1336

MADONNA AND CHILD. Panel, $35\frac{5}{8} \times 24\frac{3}{8}$ in. (85,5 × 62 cm.). Painted c. 1320. *Plates* 1–2

Provenance: Edouard de Max, Paris; Goldman Collection, New York; Samuel H. Kress Collection, 1937 (K 473).
WASHINGTON, D.C., National Gallery of Art (367).

GIOVANNI DI PAOLO
Sienese, 1403–1482

THE ANNUNCIATION. Panel, $15\frac{3}{4} \times 18\frac{1}{4}$ in. (40 × 46 cm.). Painted 1440/50. *Plates* 12–13

Provenance: Benson Collection, London; Samuel H. Kress Collection, 1936 (K 412).
WASHINGTON, D.C., National Gallery of Art (334).

JAN GOSSAERT (MABUSE)
Flemish, c. 1478–1533/36

ST. JEROME PENITENT. Two panels, oak. Each, 34 × 10 in. (86 × 25,4 cm.). *Plate* 79

Samuel H. Kress Collection, 1949 (K 1661).
WASHINGTON, D.C., National Gallery of Art (1119).

BENOZZO GOZZOLI
Florentine, 1420–1497

THE DANCE OF SALOME AND THE BEHEADING OF ST. JOHN THE BAPTIST. Panel, poplar, $9\frac{1}{4} \times 13\frac{1}{2}$ in. (23,5 × 34,5 cm.). *Plate* 26
Painted in 1461.

Provenance: Private collection, Italy; Samuel H. Kress Collection, 1949 (K 1648).
WASHINGTON, D.C., National Gallery of Art (1086).

EL GRECO
Spanish, 1541–1614

CHRIST CLEANSING THE TEMPLE. Panel, $25\frac{3}{4} \times 32\frac{3}{4}$ in. (65,4 × 83,2 cm.). *Plate* 123
Signed below on the left in Greek characters:
ΔΟΜΗΝΙΚΟΣ ΘΕΟΤΟΚΟΠΟΛΟΣ ΚΡΗΣ

Provenance: Sir Herbert Cook, Richmond, Surrey; Sir Francis Cook, Richmond, Surrey; Samuel H. Kress Collection, 1955 (K 2127).
WASHINGTON, D.C., National Gallery of Art (1482).

LAOCOÖN. Canvas, $54\frac{1}{8} \times 67\frac{7}{8}$ in. (137,5 × 172,5 cm.). *Plates* 124–126

Provenance: Estate of El Greco; Dukes of Montpensier, Seville; Palace of San Telmo, Seville (1906); Infante Don Antonio De Orleans; Sanlucar De Barrameda, Spain (1908); Durand-Ruel, Paris; E. Fischer, Charlottenburg (1914); Prince Paul of Yugoslavia, Belgrade, Serbia; Samuel H. Kress Collection, 1945 (K 1413).
WASHINGTON, D.C., National Gallery of Art (885).

MATHIS GRÜNEWALD
German, c. 1465–1528

THE SMALL CRUCIFIXION. Panel, $24\frac{1}{4} \times 18\frac{1}{8}$ in. (61,6 × 46 cm.). *Plates* 75–77
Inscribed, near the top of the cross, «m. g.».
Painted c. 1505/10.

Provenance: Duke William V of Bavaria (1605); Duke Maximilian I of Bavaria (1650); Landrat Dr. Friedrich Schöne, Essen, Germany (1922); Franz Wilhelm Koenigs, Haarlem, Holland (1927); Samuel H. Kress Collection, 1953 (K 1938). WASHINGTON, D.C., National Gallery of Art (1379).

FRANCESCO GUARDI
Venetian, 1712–1793

CAMPO SAN ZANIPOLO. Canvas, $14\frac{3}{4} \times 12\frac{3}{8}$ in. ($37,5 \times 31,5$ cm.). *Plates 163–164*
Painted 1782.

Provenance: Sir George Kane Collection, London; Samuel H. Kress Collection, 1933 (K 262).
WASHINGTON, D.C., National Gallery of Art (240).

HANS HOLBEIN, THE YOUNGER
German, 1497–1543

PORTRAIT OF A YOUNG MAN. Panel, $8\frac{5}{8} \times 6\frac{5}{8}$ in. ($21,9 \times 16,8$ cm.). *Plate 82*
Painted c. 1520.

Provenance: Baron Louis de Rothschild, Vienna, Austria; Samuel H. Kress Collection, 1952 (K 1892).
WASHINGTON, D.C., National Gallery of Art (1381).

PIETER DE HOOCH
Dutch, 1629–1684?

YOUNG MOTHER. Canvas, $26\frac{5}{8} \times 21\frac{13}{16}$ in. ($67,5 \times 55,4$ cm.).
Painted c. 1663. *Plate 146*

Provenance: Ronald Brakespeare, Esq., Henley, Oxon, England; Catherine Deere Butterworth, Moline, Illinois; Samuel H. Kress Collection, 1955 (K 2120).
SAN FRANCISCO, California, M. H. De Young Memorial Museum.

JEAN-ANTOINE HOUDON
French, 1741–1828

GIUSEPPE BALSAMO, COUNT CAGLIOSTRO. Marble (without base), $24\frac{3}{4} \times 23 \times 13\frac{1}{2}$ in. ($63 \times 58 \times 34,5$ cm.).
Signed and dated: "houdon f. 1786." *Plates 182–183*

Provenance: The Fourth Marquis of Hertford (1860); Sir Richard Wallace (1870); Lady Wallace (1890); Sir John Murray Scott, Paris (1897); Lady Sackville (1912); Samuel H. Kress Collection, 1952 (K 1907).
WASHINGTON, D.C., National Gallery of Art (A–1627).

JEAN-AUGUSTE-DOMINIQUE INGRES
French, 1780–1867

MONSIEUR MARCOTTE. Canvas, $36\frac{3}{4} \times 27\frac{1}{4}$ in. ($93,5 \times 69,3$ cm.). *Plate 185*
Signed and dated: "Ingres pinx, Rome, 1810."

Provenance: Until recently in the property of the descendants of M. Marcotte, Paris; Mme Pougin de la Maisonneuve, Paris; Samuel H. Kress Collection, 1949 (K 1650).
WASHINGTON, D.C., National Gallery of Art (1107).

MADAME MOITESSIER. Canvas, $58\frac{1}{4} \times 40$ in. (148×105 cm.). *Plates 186–187*
Signed and dated, lower left: "J. A. D. Ingres, Pixit, ANo. 1851."

Provenance: Comtesse de Flavigny; Vicomtesse O. de Bondy; Comte Olivier de Bondy; Samuel H. Kress Collection, 1945 (K 1407).
WASHINGTON, D.C., National Gallery of Art (882).

JUAN DE FLANDES
Hispano-Flemish, active 1496–c. 1519

THE ANNUNCIATION. Panel, $43\frac{1}{4} \times 31\frac{1}{4}$ in. ($109,9 \times 79,4$ cm.). *Plate 67*
Painted c. 1510.

Provenance: Parish Church of San Lázaro, Palencia, Spain; Samuel H. Kress Collection, 1953 (K 1942).
WASHINGTON, D.C., National Gallery of Art (1382).
Three further panels from the same altar-piece, also in the Kress Collection (K 1943–1945): *The Nativity, The Adoration of the Magi, The Baptism of Christ,* Washington, D.C., National Gallery of Art (1383, 1384, 1385).

NICOLAS LANCRET
French, 1690–1743

THE PICNIC AFTER THE HUNT. Canvas, $24\frac{1}{8} \times 29\frac{3}{8}$ in. ($61,5 \times 74,8$ cm.). *Plates 172–173*

Provenance: Until 1923 in the Neues Palais, Potsdam, Germany (property of the Kings of Prussia); Samuel H. Kress Collection, 1946 (K 1420).
WASHINGTON, D.C., National Gallery of Art (1105).

ROBERT LE LORRAIN
French, 1666–1743

GALATEA. Marble, $31\frac{17}{32} \times 14\frac{15}{16} \times 18\frac{7}{16}$ in. ($82,6 \times 36,7 \times 46,3$ cm.). *Plate 167–168*
Signed and dated on back of the base: "Robert Le Lorrain sculpt. 1701."

Provenance: Académie Royale, Paris; Versailles Museum (until 1819); Maréchal Family; Samuel H. Kress Collection, 1949 (K 1651).
WASHINGTON, D.C., National Gallery of Art (A–1629).

LOUIS LE NAIN
French, c. 1593–1648

A FRENCH INTERIOR. Canvas, $21\frac{7}{8} \times 25\frac{3}{8}$ in. ($55,6 \times 64,7$ cm.). *Plate 145*

Provenance: Orléans Gallery, Paris; Duke of Leeds, England; Samuel H. Kress Collection, 1946 (K 1418).
WASHINGTON, D.C., National Gallery of Art (1103).

FRA FILIPPO LIPPI
Florentine, c. 1406–1469

ST. BENEDICT ORDERS ST. MAURUS TO THE RESCUE OF ST. PLACIDUS. Panel, $16\frac{3}{8} \times 28$ in. ($41,7 \times 71,1$ cm.). *Plates 23, 25*

Provenance: Collection Cernuschi; Collection Aynard; Mrs. Douine, Château de la Boissière, Seine-et-Oise, France; Samuel H. Kress Collection, 1942 (K 1342).
WASHINGTON, D.C., National Gallery of Art (804).

PIETRO LOMBARDO
Lombard-Venetian, c. 1435–1515

A SINGING ANGEL. Marble, $33\frac{7}{8} \times 11 \times 11\frac{27}{32}$ in. ($86 \times 28 \times 30$ cm.). *Plate 49*
About 1480.

Provenance: Chabrière-Arles Collection, Lyon, France; Clarence H. Mackay, Roslyn, L. I., New York; Samuel H. Kress Collection, 1939 (K 1305).
WASHINGTON, D.C., National Gallery of Art (A–47).

LORENZO LOTTO
Venetian, c. 1480–1556

A MAIDEN'S DREAM. Panel, $16\frac{7}{8} \times 13\frac{1}{4}$ in. (43×34 cm.).
Painted c. 1505. *Plate 90*

Provenance: Collection of Lord Conway, London, England; Samuel H. Kress Collection, 1934 (K 291).
WASHINGTON, D.C., National Gallery of Art (258).

PORTRAIT OF A BEARDED MAN. Canvas, $38\frac{1}{2} \times 33\frac{1}{2}$ in. ($97,8 \times 85,1$ cm.). *Plate 91*
Painted c. 1525.

Provenance: Prince Giovannelli, Venice, Italy; Samuel H. Kress Collection, 1932 (K 208).
NEW ORLEANS, Louisiana, The Isaac Delgado Museum of Art.

BERNARDINO LUINI
Milanese, c. 1480–1532

THE MAGDALEN. Panel (poplar), $23\frac{1}{8} \times 19$ in. ($58,7 \times 48,3$ cm.). *Plate 96*

Provenance: Henry, 3rd Marquess of Lansdowne, Bowood Park, Calne, Wiltshire, England; Henry, 4th Marquess of Lansdowne; Henry Charles Keith, 5th Marquess of Lansdowne; Henry William Edmund, 6th Marquess of Lansdowne; Samuel H. Kress Collection, 1957 (K 2159).
WASHINGTON, D.C., National Gallery of Art (1608).

ALESSANDRO MAGNASCO
Genoese, 1667–1749

PULCINELLA SINGING WITH HIS MANY CHILDREN AND A LUTE-PLAYER. Canvas, 30×41 in. ($76,2 \times 104,1$ cm.). *Plate 154*
Painted between 1711 and 1735.

Provenance: Private Collection in Germany; bought in England for the Samuel H. Kress Collection, 1953 (K 1952).
COLUMBIA, South Carolina, The Columbia Museum of Art.

THE BAPTISM OF CHRIST. Canvas, $46\frac{1}{4} \times 57\frac{3}{4}$ in. (117×147 cm.). *Plates 155, 157*
Painted c. 1730.

Provenance: Private Collection, Genoa, Italy; Sambon Collection, Paris; Samuel H. Kress Collection, 1939 (K 1191).
WASHINGTON, National Gallery of Art (528).

ANDREA MANTEGNA
Paduan, 1431–1506

PORTRAIT OF A MAN. Panel, $9\frac{1}{2} \times 7\frac{1}{2}$ in. ($24,3 \times 19,1$ cm.). *Plate 41*

Provenance: Private Family in Balaton Boglar, Hungary (until 1906); Dr. Ludwig Keleman, Budapest, Hungary (until 1929); Samuel H. Kress Collection, 1950 (K 1709).
WASHINGTON, D.C., National Gallery of Art (1088).

QUENTIN MASSYS
Flemish, 1465/66–1530

ST. CHRISTOPHER. Panel, $26\frac{1}{4} \times 19$ in. ($66,7 \times 48,3$ cm.).
Painted c. 1490. *Plate 69*

Provenance: Dr. von Cranach, Wartburg, Thuringen, Germany; Samuel H. Kress Collection, 1952 (K 1903).
ALLENTOWN, Pennsylvania, Allentown Art Museum.

HANS MEMLING
Flemish, c. 1430/35–1494

ST. VERONICA (Obv.); CHALICE OF ST. JOHN THE EVANGELIST (Rev.). Panel, $12\frac{1}{4} \times 9\frac{1}{2}$ in. ($31,1 \times 24,2$ cm.). *Plates 55–56*

Provenance: Prince Nicolas de Demidoff, San Donato (Florence), Italy; Private Collection, Florence; Baron Thyssen, Schloss Rohoncz, Lugano, Switzerland; Samuel H. Kress Collection, 1951 (K 1840).
WASHINGTON, D.C., National Gallery of Art (1125).

THE PRESENTATION IN THE TEMPLE. Panel, $23\frac{1}{2} \times 19$ in. ($59,8 \times 48,3$ cm.). *Plates 57–58 and frontispiece*
Painted c. 1463.

Provenance: Count Johann Rudolf Czernin von Chudenitz, Vienna, Austria; Czernin Gallery, Vienna; Samuel H. Kress Collection, 1955 (K 2088).
WASHINGTON, D.C., National Gallery of Art (1389).

MORETTO DA BRESCIA
Brescian, c. 1498–1554

PIETÀ. Panel, $69\frac{1}{8} \times 38\frac{3}{4}$ in. ($175,8 \times 98,5$ cm.). *Plates 94–95*
Painted in the 1520s.

Provenance: The Earl of Egremont; Cook Collection, Richmond, Surrey; Samuel H. Kress Collection, 1947 (K 1428).
WASHINGTON, D.C., National Gallery of Art (1093).

JEAN-MARC NATTIER
French, 1685–1766

JOSEPH BONNIER DE LA MOSSON. Canvas, $54\frac{1}{4} \times 41\frac{1}{2}$ in. ($137,9 \times 105,4$ cm.). *Plate 175*
Signed and dated on the base of the column at left: "Nattier 1745."

Provenance: G. Rothan, Paris; Samuel H. Kress Collection, 1954 (K 2041).
WASHINGTON, D.C., National Gallery of Art (1391).

NINO PISANO
Pisan, mentioned 1347–1368

THE VIRGIN ANNUNCIATE AND THE ARCHANGEL GABRIEL. Wood, polychromed and gilded.   *Plates* 5–6
The Archangel: $62\frac{3}{4} \times 18\frac{5}{8} \times 14\frac{1}{8}$ in. (without base), $159,4 \times 47,3 \times 36$ cm.
The Virgin: $63\frac{7}{8} \times 21\frac{3}{8} \times 15\frac{1}{2}$ in. (without base), $162,5 \times 54,5 \times 39,4$ cm.
Datable between 1360 and 1368.

Provenance: Private Collection, Italy; Rush H. Kress, New York; Samuel H. Kress Collection, 1950 (K 600, K 601).
WASHINGTON, D.C., National Gallery of Art (A–1632, A–1633).

PAOLO VENEZIANO
Venetian, active 1321–1358

THE CORONATION OF THE VIRGIN. Panel, $39 \times 30\frac{1}{2}$ in. (99,1 × 77,5 cm.).   *Plate* 3
Dated, at lower center: MCCCXXIIII (1324).

Provenance: Dal Zotto, Venice; Samuel H. Kress Collection, 1952 (K 1895).
WASHINGTON, D.C., National Gallery of Art (1166).

JEAN-BAPTISTE-JOSEPH PATER
French, 1695–1736

FÊTE CHAMPÊTRE. Canvas, $29\frac{3}{8} \times 36\frac{1}{2}$ in. (74,5 × 92,5 cm.).
Plates 170–171

Provenance: Mme la Baronne Wilhelm von Rothschild, Schloss Grüneburg, Frankfurt am Main, Germany; Samuel H. Kress Collection, 1945 (K 1408).
WASHINGTON, D.C., National Gallery of Art (883).

GIOVANNI BATTISTA PIAZZETTA
Venetian, 1682–1754

ELIJAH TAKEN UP IN A CHARIOT OF FIRE. Canvas, $68\frac{3}{4} \times 104\frac{1}{4}$ in. (174,6 × 264,8 cm.).   *Plate* 159

Provenance: Pivan Collection, Venice, Italy; Samuel H. Kress Collection, 1950 (K 1810).
WASHINGTON, D.C., National Gallery of Art (1149).

NICOLAS POUSSIN
French, 1593/4–1665

THE HOLY FAMILY ON THE STEPS. Canvas, $27 \times 38\frac{1}{2}$ in. (68,6 × 97,8 cm.).   *Plate* 130
Painted in 1648.

Provenance: Duke of Sutherland, Stafford House, England; Samuel H. Kress Collection, 1949 (K 1642).
WASHINGTON, D.C., National Gallery of Art (1128).

JACOPO DELLA QUERCIA
Sienese, 1367(?)–1438

MADONNA OF HUMILITY. Marble, $22\frac{31}{32} \times 19\frac{1}{4} \times 11\frac{1}{8}$ in. (58,4 × 48,8 × 28,3 cm.).   *Plate* 8

Provenance: Prince Hercolani, Bologna, Italy; Henry Goldman, New York; Samuel H. Kress Collection, 1944 (K 1384).
WASHINGTON, D.C., National Gallery of Art (A–157).

RAPHAEL (RAFFAELLO SANTI)
Umbrian, 1483–1520

BINDO ALTOVITI. Panel, $23\frac{1}{2} \times 17\frac{1}{4}$ in. (60 × 44 cm.).
Painted c. 1513.   *Plates* 97–98

Provenance: In the Altoviti Palace, Florence, until 1808; Ludwig of Bavaria (later King Ludwig I); Alte Pinakothek, Munich; Samuel H. Kress Collection, 1940 (K 1239).
WASHINGTON, D.C., National Gallery of Art (534).

SEBASTIANO RICCI
Venetian, 1659–1734

THE BATTLE OF THE CENTAURS AND LAPITHS. Canvas, $54\frac{1}{2} \times 69\frac{5}{8}$ in. (138,5 × 177 cm.).   *Plate* 156
Painted c. 1723.

Provenance: Sir Richard Coulthurst, Bart., Blarney Castle, Cork, Ireland; Samuel H. Kress Collection, 1953 (K 1955).
ATLANTA, Georgia, Atlanta Art Association Galleries.

SEBASTIANO and MARCO RICCI
Venetians: SR, 1659–1734 MR, 1676–1729

MEMORIAL TO ADMIRAL SIR CLOWDISLEY SHOVELL. Canvas, $87\frac{1}{2} \times 62\frac{1}{2}$ in. (222,3 × 158,8 cm.).   *Plates* 150–151
Signed by both artists on a stone toward lower left: "B(astian). M(arco). RICCI Faciebant".
Painted between 1723 and 1729.

Provenance: Sir Richard Coulthurst, Bart., Blarney Castle, Cork, Ireland; Samuel H. Kress Collection, 1953 (K 1956).
WASHINGTON, D.C., National Gallery of Art (1610).

ERCOLE ROBERTI
Ferrarese, c. 1456–1496

GIOVANNI II BENTIVOGLIO. Panel, $21\frac{1}{8} \times 15$ in. (54 × 38 cm.).   *Plate* 43
Painted c. 1480.

Provenance: Dreyfus Collection, Paris; Samuel H. Kress Collection, 1936 (K 408).
WASHINGTON, D.C., National Gallery of Art (330).

GINEVRA BENTIVOGLIO. Panel, $21\frac{1}{8} \times 15\frac{1}{4}$ in. (54 × 39 cm.).
Painted c. 1480.   *Plate* 44

Provenance: Dreyfus Collection, Paris; Samuel H. Kress Collection, 1936 (K 409).
WASHINGTON, D.C., National Gallery of Art (331).

ROMANINO (GIROLAMO ROMANI)
Brescian, 1484/87–1562/66

THE MYSTIC MARRIAGE OF ST. CATHERINE. Canvas, $60\frac{1}{4} \times 81\frac{3}{4}$ in. ($153 \times 207,7$ cm.).   *Plate* 93
Painted c. 1530.

Provenance: Erizzo-Maffei Collection, Brescia, Italy; Sir Francis Cook, Richmond, Surrey; Sir Herbert Cook, Bart., Richmond, Surrey; Samuel H. Kress Collection, 1948 (K 1551).
MEMPHIS, Tennessee, Brooks Memorial Art Gallery.

ANTONIO ROSSELLINO
Florentine, 1427–1478/79

THE YOUNG SAINT JOHN THE BAPTIST. Marble, $13\frac{5}{8} \times 11\frac{3}{4} \times 6\frac{11}{32}$ in. ($34,7 \times 29,8 \times 16,1$ cm.).   *Plate* 33
Datable between 1470 and 1475.

Provenance: Church of San Francesco dei Vanchetoni, Florence, Italy; Samuel H. Kress Collection, 1941 (K 1252).
WASHINGTON, D.C., National Gallery of Art (A–54).

ROSSO FIORENTINO
Florentine, 1494–1540

PORTRAIT OF A MAN. Panel, $34\frac{1}{4} \times 26\frac{1}{4}$ in. ($87 \times 66,8$ cm.).
Painted c. 1523.   *Plate* 99
Samuel H. Kress Collection, 1950 (K 1735).
WASHINGTON, D.C., National Gallery of Art (1611).

PETER PAUL RUBENS
Flemish, 1577–1640

PORTRAIT OF MARCHESA BRIGIDA SPINOLA DORIA. Canvas, $60 \times 37\frac{7}{8}$ in. ($152,4 \times 98,8$ cm.).   *Plates* 135–136
Painted in 1606.

Provenance: The Doria Family, Genoa, Italy; Marchese Gian Vincenzo Imperiali (1648), Genoa; Marchese Francesco Maria Imperiali (1661), Genoa; General Sir John Murray, Bart., G.C.B. (1827), Clermont, Fifeshire, Scotland; Simon Horsin-Déon (1867), Paris; Charles J. Nieuwenhuys (1886), Brussels; Charles Wertheimer, London; Samuel H. Kress Collection, 1957 (K 2187).
WASHINGTON, D.C., National Gallery of Art (1612).

THE LAST SUPPER. Oak panel, $17\frac{1}{8} \times 17\frac{1}{4}$ in. ($43,5 \times 43,8$ cm.).   *Plate* 137
Painted in 1620/21.

Provenance: Jacques de Roore, The Hague, Holland (1747); Jacques Clemens, Ghent (1779); Marquise d'Aoust, Paris (1924); Francesco Gentili di Giuseppe, Paris; Samuel H. Kress Collection, 1954 (K 1997).
SEATTLE, Washington, Seattle Art Museum.

DECIUS MUS ADDRESSING THE LEGIONS. Panel, $31\frac{3}{4} \times 33\frac{1}{4}$ in. ($80,7 \times 84,5$ cm.).   *Plate* 138
Painted 1617.

Provenance: Randon de Boisset, Paris; Lebrun, Paris; Fritz August von Kaulbach, Munich, Germany (1929); Samuel H. Kress Collection, 1955 (K 2117).
WASHINGTON, D.C., National Gallery of Art (1394).

PIETER JANSZ. SAENREDAM
Dutch, 1597–1665

CHURCH OF SANTA MARIA DELLA FEBBRE, ROME. Panel, $14\frac{7}{8} \times 27\frac{3}{4}$ in. ($37,8 \times 70,5$ cm.).   *Plate* 149
Signed and dated on the lower part of the obelisk shaft. "P. Saenreda fe Ao 1629".

Provenance: Frederick the Great of Prussia; A. W. M. Mensing, Amsterdam; Jonkheer J. A. G. Sandberg, Wassenaar, near Leiden; Private Dutch Collection; Samuel H. Kress Collection, 1954 (K 1999).
WASHINGTON, D.C., National Gallery of Art (1396).

SALVIATI (FRANCESCO DE' ROSSI)
Florentine, 1510–1563

BUST PORTRAIT OF A YOUNG MAN. Panel, $23\frac{1}{8} \times 18\frac{1}{4}$ in. ($58,8 \times 46,3$ cm.).   *Plate* 100
Painted c. 1539/40.

Provenance: Ferroni Collection, Florence, Italy; Samuel H. Kress Collection, 1935 (K 339).
HONOLULU, Hawaii, The Honolulu Academy of Arts.

SASSETTA and Assistant
Sienese, active 1423–1450

THE MEETING OF ST. ANTHONY AND ST. PAUL. Panel, $18\frac{3}{4} \times 13\frac{5}{8}$ in. ($47,5 \times 34,5$ cm.).   *Plates* 17–18
Painted c. 1432/36.

Provenance: Lord Allendale, London; Samuel H. Kress Collection, 1938 (K 513).
WASHINGTON, D.C., National Gallery of Art (404).

GIOVANNI GIROLAMO SAVOLDO
Brescian, active 1508–1548

PORTRAIT OF A KNIGHT. Canvas, $34\frac{3}{4} \times 28\frac{7}{8}$ in. ($88,3 \times 73,4$ cm.).   *Plate* 92

Provenance: Prince Liechtenstein, Vaduz, Liechtenstein; Samuel H. Kress Collection, 1951 (K 1846).
WASHINGTON, D.C., National Gallery of Art (1153).

MARTIN SCHAFFNER
German, c. 1480–1541

PORTRAIT OF A LADY OF THE PATRICIAN FAMILY SCHAD VON MITTELBIBERACH. Panel, pinewood, $37\frac{3}{8} \times 28\frac{7}{8}$ in. ($95 \times 73,3$ cm.).   *Plate* 83

Provenance: The Family Schad von Mittelbiberach, Ulm, Germany; Count Leutrum Collection; Prof. H. Freiherr von Habermann, Munich, Germany; Rodolphe Kann Collection, Paris; Samuel H. Kress Collection, 1957 (K 2172).
DENVER, Colorado, Denver Art Museum.

SEBASTIANO DEL PIOMBO
Venetian, c. 1485–1547

PORTRAIT OF A HUMANIST. Panel, 52×39 in. (132×99 cm.).   *Plates* 109–110
Painted c. 1520.

Provenance: Ghizzi Gamily, Naples, Italy; Henry, 3rd Marquess of Lansdowne, Bowood Park, Calne, Wiltshire, England; Henry, 4th Marquess of Lansdowne; Henry Charles Keith, 5th Marquess of Lansdowne; Henry William Edmund, 6th Marquess of Lansdowne; Samuel H. Kress Collection, 1955 (K 2115).
WASHINGTON, D.C., National Gallery of Art (1400).

SODOMA (GIOVANNI ANTONIO BAZZI)
Sienese, 1477–1549

ST. GEORGE AND THE DRAGON. Panel, $55\frac{1}{2}×38\frac{3}{8}$ in. (137,8×97,6 cm.).   *Plates* 101–102
Provenance: The Earl of Shrewsbury; Cook Collection, Richmond, Surrey; Samuel H. Kress Collection, 1947 (K 1426).
WASHINGTON, D.C., National Gallery of Art (1155).

MASSIMO STANZIONE
Neapolitan, 1585–1656

THE ASSUMPTION OF THE VIRGIN. Canvas, $108\frac{1}{2}×74\frac{5}{8}$ in. (275,6×190 cm.).   *Plate* 127
Provenance: Sir Henry Wellesley, Lord Cowley; Cook Collection, Richmond, Surrey; Samuel H. Kress Collection, 1955 (K 2112).
RALEIGH, North Carolina, North Carolina Museum of Art.

BERNARDO STROZZI
Genoese-Venetian, 1581–1644

ST. LAWRENCE GIVING THE TREASURES OF THE CHURCH TO THE POOR. Canvas, $38\frac{1}{2}×52\frac{11}{16}$ in. (97,9×134 cm.).   *Plates* 147–148
Provenance: Sir C. R. Bourchier Wrey, Bart., Tavestock Court, Barnstaple, North Devon, England; Samuel H. Kress Collection, 1950 (K 1693).
PORTLAND, Oregon, Portland Art Museum.

TANZIO DA VARALLO
Lombard, c. 1575–1635

ST. JOHN THE BAPTIST IN THE WILDERNESS. Canvas, $63\frac{3}{4}×43\frac{3}{4}$ in. (161,9×111,2 cm.).   *Plate* 128
Painted c. 1616.

Provenance: Enrico Marinucci Collection, Rome, Italy; Samuel H. Kress Collection, 1939 (K 1223).
TULSA, Oklahoma, Philbrook Art Center.

GIOVANNI BATTISTA TIEPOLO
Venetian, 1696–1770

APOLLO PURSUING DAPHNE. Canvas, 27×34 in. (68,8×87,2 cm.).   *Plate* 160
Signed at the lower left: "J. B. Tiepolo".
Painted in the 1750s.

Provenance: Edward Kann Collection, Paris; Madame Delaney, Paris; Pierre Lauth, Paris; Samuel H. Kress Collection, 1950 (K 1836).
WASHINGTON, D.C., National Gallery of Art (1157).

JACOPO TINTORETTO
Venetian, 1518–1594

DOGE ALVISE MOCENIGO AND FAMILY BEFORE THE MADONNA AND CHILD. Canvas, $85×163\frac{1}{2}$ in. (215,9×415,3 cm.).   *Plates* 120–121
Painted 1573.

Provenance: Tommaso Mocenigo, Venice (1648); Marquess Hippolythe de Gouvello, Brittany, France; Samuel H. Kress Collection, 1953 (K 1964).
WASHINGTON, D.C., National Gallery of Art (1406).

TITIAN (TIZIANO VECELLIO)
Venetian, c. 1477–1576

RANUCCIO FARNESE. Canvas, $35\frac{3}{8}×29$ in. (89,9×73,7 cm.). Signed: TITIANUS. F.   *Plates* 113, 115
Before 1542.

Provenance: Cook Collection, Richmond, Surrey, England; Samuel H. Kress Collection, 1948 (K 1562).
WASHINGTON, D.C., National Gallery of Art (1094).

DOGE ANDREA GRITTI. Canvas, $51\frac{1}{2}×41\frac{1}{2}$ in. (130×105,4 cm.).   *Plates* 114, 116
Signed at right: TITIANUS E. F.
Between 1535 and 1540.

Provenance: King Charles I of England (from 1626); Wenzel Anton Prinz Kaunitz-Rietberg (till 1820); Count Johann Rudolf Czernin von Chudenitz, Vienna, Austria; Samuel H. Kress Collection, 1954 (K 2040).
WASHINGTON, D.C., National Gallery of Art (1408).

ST. JOHN THE EVANGELIST ON PATMOS. Canvas, $93\frac{1}{2}×103\frac{1}{2}$ in. (237,6×263 cm.).   *Plate* 117
Painted c. 1530/35.

Provenance: Accademia, Venice (until 1818); Private Collection, Turin, Italy; Samuel H. Kress Collection, 1954 (K 2066).
WASHINGTON, D.C., National Gallery of Art (1484).

GASPARE TRAVERSI
Neapolitan, 1749–1769

THE ARTS—MUSIC. Canvas, $59\frac{5}{8}×80\frac{3}{8}$ in. (151,5×205 cm.). Signed at the lower left: "Gaspar Traversi P."   *Plate* 152
Painted c. 1760.

Provenance: R. Herzka, Vienna, Austria; Samuel H. Kress Collection, 1933 (K 1957).
KANSAS CITY, Missouri, The William Rockhill Nelson Gallery and Mary Atkins Museum of Fine Arts.

Companion piece, also in the Kress Collection (K 1958): *The Arts—Drawing*, Kansas City, Missouri, The William Rockhill Nelson Gallery and Mary Atkins Museum of Fine Arts.

COSIMO TURA
Ferrarese, c. 1430–1495

MADONNA AND CHILD IN A GARDEN. Panel, $20\frac{3}{4} \times 14\frac{5}{8}$ in. (53×37 cm.). *Plate* 47

Provenance: Harold I. Pratt, New York, N.Y.; Samuel H. Kress Collection, 1943 (K 1373).
WASHINGTON, D.C., National Gallery of Art (827).

PAOLO VERONESE
Venetian, 1528–1588

THE ANNUNCIATION. Canvas, $38\frac{3}{4} \times 29\frac{5}{8}$ in. ($98,4 \times 75,3$ cm.). *Plate* 118
Painted c. 1583.

Provenance: Collection of the Duke of Westminster, London; Mr. Julius H. Haass, Detroit, Mich.; Mrs. Lilian Henkel Haass, Detroit, Mich.; Samuel H. Kress Collection, 1957 (K 2169).
WASHINGTON, D.C., National Gallery of Art (1529).

REBECCA AT THE WELL. Canvas, $57\frac{1}{4} \times 111\frac{1}{4}$ in. ($145,5 \times 282,7$ cm.). *Plate* 119
Painted c. 1580.

Provenance: George Villiers, First Duke of Buckingham; George Villiers, Second Duke of Buckingham, England; Archduke Leopold Wilhelm, Prague; Gemäldegalerie, Vienna, Austria; Samuel H. Kress Collection, 1952 (K 1898).
WASHINGTON, D.C., National Gallery of Art (1161).

ANDREA DEL VERROCCHIO
Florentine, 1435–1488

LORENZO DE' MEDICI. Terracotta, painted, $25\frac{7}{8} \times 23\frac{1}{4} \times 12\frac{7}{8}$ in. ($65,8 \times 59 \times 32,8$ cm.). *Plate* 39

Provenance: Emilio Santarelli, Florence, Italy; E. Nicholl Dennys, London; Henry Labouchere, London; Lord Taunton, London (1850); Hon. Edward A. Vessey Stanley, Bridgewater, England; Clarence H. Mackay, Roslyn, L.I., New York; Samuel H. Kress Collection, 1941 (K 1277).
WASHINGTON, D.C., National Gallery of Art (A–146).

CIRCLE OF VERROCCHIO
Florentine School, c. 1475

MADONNA AND CHILD WITH A POMEGRANATE. Panel, $6\frac{1}{4} \times 5$ in. ($15,7 \times 12,8$ cm.). *Plate* 34

Provenance: John Watkins Brett, London; Charles Timbal, Paris; Gustave Dreyfus, Paris; Samuel H. Kress Collection, 1951 (K 1850).
WASHINGTON, D.C., National Gallery of Art (1144).

PETER VISCHER, THE YOUNGER
German, 1487–1528

ORPHEUS AND EURYDICE. Bronze, $8 \times 5\frac{21}{32}$ in. ($20,3 \times 14,4$ cm.). *Plate* 80

Provenance: Gustave Dreyfus, Paris; Samuel H. Kress Collection, 1944 (K 1379.431B).
WASHINGTON, D.C., National Gallery of Art (A–709.431B).

ALESSANDRO VITTORIA
Venetian, 1525–1608

PORTRAIT OF A YOUNG KNIGHT. Terracotta, $35\frac{7}{8} \times 24 \times 12\frac{3}{4}$ in. ($91,3 \times 61 \times 32,9$ cm.). *Plate* 122
Datable 1590/1600.

Provenance: Palazzo Carregiani (formerly Zorzi), Venice, Italy (1854); Österreichisches Museum für Kunst und Industrie, Vienna, Austria (1866); Samuel H. Kress Collection, 1954 (K 1983).
WASHINGTON, D.C., National Gallery of Art (A–1666).

SIMON VOUET
French, 1590–1649

THE MUSES URANIA AND CALLIOPE. Panel, oak, $31\frac{3}{8} \times 49\frac{3}{8}$ in. ($79,8 \times 125$ cm.). *Plate* 132
Samuel H. Kress Collection, 1957 (2177).
WASHINGTON, D.C., National Gallery of Art (1613).

ST. JEROME AND THE ANGEL. Canvas, $56\frac{7}{8} \times 71$ in. ($144,6 \times 180,3$ cm.). *Plate* 133
Painted before 1620.

Provenance: Galleria Barberini, Rome, Italy; Samuel H. Kress Collection, 1952 (K 1891).
WASHINGTON, D.C., National Gallery of Art (1415).

ANTOINE WATTEAU
French, 1684–1721

CERES. Canvas, $54\frac{1}{2} \times 49\frac{1}{2}$ in. ($138,5 \times 125,8$ cm.). *Plate* 166
Painted c. 1712.

Provenance: Crozat Mansion, Paris; Lebrun, Paris; H. A. J. Munro, Novar, Scotland; Charles Sedelmeyer, Paris (1895); Sir Lionel Phillips, Tylner Hall, Winchfield, England; H. Michel-Lévy, Paris; Charles-Louis Dreyfus, Paris; Samuel H. Kress Collection, 1954 (K 2048).
WASHINGTON, D.C., National Gallery of Art (1413).

MARCO ZOPPO
Ferrarese, 1433–c. 1478

MADONNA AND CHILD. Panel, $15\frac{3}{8} \times 11\frac{5}{8}$ in. ($40 \times 29,6$ cm.). *Plate* 46

Signed on the parapet: MARCO ZOPPO DA BOLOGNA / OPVS.
Painted c. 1470.

Provenance: Cook Collection, Richmond, Surrey; Samuel H. Kress Collection, 1954 (K 2033).
WASHINGTON, D.C., National Gallery of Art (1414).

FRANCISCO DE ZURBARAN
Spanish, 1598–1664

ST. JEROME WITH ST. PAULA AND ST. EUSTOCHIUM. Canvas, $96\frac{1}{2} \times 68\frac{1}{8}$ in. ($245,1 \times 173$ cm.).
Painted c. 1640. *Plate* 134

Provenance: Frank Hall Standish; King Louis-Philippe, Louvre, Paris (1842); Alphonse Oudry, Paris; Samuel H. Kress Collection, 1952 (K 1896).
WASHINGTON, D.C., National Gallery of Art (1167).

MASTER OF THE BARBERINI PANELS
Umbrian, 15th Century

THE ANNUNCIATION. Panel, $34\frac{1}{2} \times 24\frac{3}{4}$ in. (88×63 cm.). Painted c. 1450. *Plate 27*

Provenance: Dreyfus Collection, Paris; Samuel H. Kress Collection, 1936 (K 407).
WASHINGTON, D.C., National Gallery of Art (329).

FLORENTINE PAINTER, XVI CENTURY

ALLEGORICAL PORTRAIT OF DANTE. Panel (poplar), $50 \times 47\frac{1}{4}$ in. ($127 \times 121,5$ cm.). page 3

Provenance: Graham Collection, London; Lord Hailsham, London; Samuel H. Kress Collection, 1956 (K 2154).
WASHINGTON, D.C., National Gallery of Art (1609).

MASTER OF FLÉMALLE and Assistants
Flemish, first half of 15th Century

MADONNA AND CHILD WITH SAINTS IN THE EN-CLOSED GARDEN. Panel, oak, $47\frac{1}{8} \times 58\frac{1}{2}$ in. ($119,7 \times 148,6$ cm.). *Plates 9–11*

Provenance: M. Imbert des Motellettes (1833); De Potter-Soenbut, Bruges, Belgium (1843); Comtesse d'Oudemard; Samuel H. Kress Collection, 1949 (K 1646).
WASHINGTON, D.C., National Gallery of Art (1388).

MASTER OF HEILIGENKREUZ
Franco-Austrian, early 15th Century

THE DEATH OF SAINT CLARE. Panel, $26\frac{1}{8} \times 21\frac{3}{8}$ in. ($66,4 \times 54,5$ cm.). *Plate 16*
Painted c. 1410 (or 1420/30).

Provenance: Private Collection in Northeast Germany; Professor Walter Schnakenberg (1936); Dr. Carl Langbehn, Munich (1951); Samuel H. Kress Collection, 1951 (K 1859).
WASHINGTON, D.C., National Gallery of Art (1162).

MASTER OF THE RETABLE
OF THE REYES CATOLICOS
Spanish, late 15th Century

THE VISITATION. Panel (pine wood), $60 \times 36\frac{7}{8}$ in. ($152,4 \times 93,7$ cm.). *Plate 65*

Provenance: Mr. John North Willys, Palm Beach, Florida; Samuel H. Kress Collection, 1951 (K 1860).
TUCSON, Arizona, The University of Arizona.

THE ADORATION OF THE MAGI. Panel (pine wood), $60\frac{3}{8} \times 36\frac{3}{4}$ in. ($153,3 \times 93,4$ cm.). *Plate 66*

Provenance: Mr. John North Willys, Palm Beach, Florida; Samuel H. Kress Collection, 1951 (K 1863).
DENVER, Colorado, Denver Art Museum.

Six further panels from the same retable, also in the Kress Collection (K 1680, 1681, 1860–1863): *The Marriage at Cana, Christ among the Doctors*, Washington, D.C., National Gallery of Art (1121–1122); *The Visitation*, Tucson, Arizona, Uni-versity of Arizona; *The Annunciation, The Adoration of the Child*, San Francisco, California, M. H. De Young Memorial Museum; *The Adoration of the Magi*, Denver, Colorado, Denver Art Museum.

MASTER OF ST. GILLES
Franco-Flemish, c. 1500

THE CONVERSION OF AN ARIAN BY ST. RÉMY. Panel, $24\frac{1}{4} \times 18$ in. ($61,6 \times 45,8$ cm.). *Plate 59*

THE BAPTISM OF CLOVIS. Panel, $24\frac{1}{4} \times 18\frac{3}{8}$ in. ($61,6 \times 46,7$ cm.). *Plate 60*

Provenance: Comte Alexandre de Lestang-Parade, Aix-en-Provence, France; Baron E. de Beurnonville, Paris; M. Watil, Paris; Samuel H. Kress Collection, 1946 (K 1421, K 1422).
WASHINGTON, D.C., National Gallery of Art (1097, 1098).

MASTER OF THE ST. LUCY LEGEND
Flemish, active 1480–1489

MARY, QUEEN OF HEAVEN. Panel, 85×73 in. ($215,9 \times 185,4$ cm.). *Plates 61–62*

Provenance: From a Convent near Burgos, Spain; Samuel H. Kress Collection, 1949 (K 1689).
WASHINGTON, D.C., National Gallery of Art (1096).

MASTER OF ST. VERONICA
School of Cologne, active early 15th Century

THE CRUCIFIXION. Panel, $16\frac{1}{8} \times 10$ in. ($41 \times 25,4$ cm.). Painted c. 1400/10. *Plate 15*

Provenance: Dr. Richard von Schnitzler, Cologne, Germany; Samuel H. Kress Collection, 1954 (K 2000).
WASHINGTON, D.C., National Gallery of Art (1390).

FRENCH PAINTER
Early 15th Century

CHRIST APPEARS TO SAINT MARY MAGDALEN AFTER HIS RESURRECTION. Transferred to masonite, $40\frac{3}{8} \times 19\frac{1}{2}$ in. ($102,5 \times 49,5$ cm.). *Plate 14*

Provenance: Private Collection, Spain; Samuel H. Kress Collection, 1952 (K 1995).
SAN FRANCISCO, California, M. H. De Young Memorial Museum.
Companion piece, also in the Kress Collection (K 1194): *The Resurrection of Christ*, San Francisco, California, M. H. De Young Memorial Museum.

FRENCH SCULPTOR
Second half of the 15th Century

ST. CHRISTOPHER. Marble, 44 in. (101,8 cm.) (including base). *Plate 68*

Provenance: Colignon Collection, Paris; Samuel H. Kress Collection, 1953 (K 1975).
PORTLAND, Oregon, Portland Art Museum.

*